Public Planet Books

A series edited by Dilip Gaonkar, Jane Kramer,
Benjamin Lee, and Michael Warner

Public Planet Books is a series designed by writers in and outside the academy—writers working on what could be called
narratives of public culture—to explore questions that urgently
concern us all. It is an attempt to open the scholarly discourse
on contemporary public culture, both local and international,
and to illuminate that discourse with the kinds of narrative
that will challenge sophisticated readers, make them think,
and especially make them question. It is, most importantly,
an experiment in strategies of discourse, combining reportage
and critical reflection on unfolding issues and events—one, we
hope, that will provide a running narrative of our societies at
this moment. Public Planet Books is part of the Public Works
publication project of the Center for Transcultural Studies,
which also includes the journal *Public Culture* and the Public
Worlds book series.

Islam and Secularity

public planet books

Islam and Secularity

The Future of Europe's Public Sphere

Nilüfer Göle

DUKE UNIVERSITY PRESS *Durham and London* 2015

Typeset in Kepler by Tseng Information Systems, Inc.

Library of Congress Cataloging-in-Publication Data
Göle, Nilüfer, [date]–author.
Islam and secularity : the future of Europe's public sphere / Nilüfer Göle.
Pages cm—(Public planet books)
Includes bibliographical references and index.
ISBN 978-0-8223-5955-5 (hardcover : alk. paper)
ISBN 978-0-8223-5998-2 (pbk. : alk. paper)
ISBN 978-0-8223-7513-5 (e-book)
1. Islam and secularism—Europe. 2. Islam and secularism—Turkey.
3. Islam—Europe. I. Title. II. Series: Public planet books.
BP190.5.S35G65 2015
306.6'97094—dc23
2015017938

Cover art: Alena Stoyko / Alamy

Contents

viii

Acknowledgments

I t is rare to associate a conference with a good fortune. For most of us, traveling for conferences has become not only a banality but also a burden. However, there are some precious moments in one's academic history that yield unexpected consequences. In 1994, a conference in which I participated in Honolulu, Hawaii, at the East-West Center, was such a moment. I owe special thanks to Dru Gladney for inviting me. I was part of a panel on secularism, a subject at that time still very marginal, even for this conference. Rajeev Bhargava, Charles Taylor, and I were the three speakers on the panel. The conference proved to be the beginning of a very fruitful collaboration. During all these years, in spite of geographical distances, we succeeded in establishing a dialogue, with the help of an extra-institutional platform provided by the Center for Transnational Cultural Studies and the journal *Public Culture*. Ben Lee, Dilip Gaonkar, Craig Calhoun, Michael Warner, and Ackbar Abbas made possible this journey toward uncharted paths of thinking and unconventional ways of exchange. Themes around public sphere, secularism, and alternative modernities brought different people from different continents together. I was lucky to be part of these circles and to share my thoughts in regard to Europe and Turkey. Working on a series of paradoxical figures and formations, secularism and sexuality, Islam and visibility, public sphere and intimacy, I was struggling for readings of modernity both from within and from the "non west." I was fortunate to have this comradeship.

My annual seminar, at École des hautes études en sciences sociales in Paris since 2001, constituted another circle, with my graduate students and colleagues, for exploring the emergence of the question of Islam in secular France.

Some of the chapters were based on the research results of my European-scale project, "EuroPublicIslam: Islam in the making of a European Public Sphere." Awarded an Advanced Grant for exceptional established research leaders, the Euro-PublicIslam project has received funding from the European Research Council under the European Community's Seventh Framework Programme from the end of 2008 to March 2013 (FP7/2007–2013/Grant Agreement no. 230244). My special thanks go to the European Research Council for the financial support it provided.

Some of the chapters have been published in different journals and edited volumes. I am grateful to Duke University Press for giving me the opportunity to bring together many of the articles on secularism in a collected volume. I benefited greatly from the remarks of the readers to improve the framework and to reorganize the content. An earlier version of chapter 2 was published under the title "European Self-Presentations and Narratives Challenged by Islam: Secular Modernity in Question," in

Decolonising European Sociology: Transdisciplinary Approaches, edited by Encarnación Gutiérrez-Rodríguez, Manuela Boatca, and Sérgio Costa (Ashgate, 2010). Chapter 3 is a revised version of "Manifestations of the Religious-Secular Divide: Self, State, and the Public Sphere," published in *Comparative Secularism in a Global Age*, edited by Linell E. Cady and Elizabeth Shakman-Hurd (Palgrave Macmillan, 2010). Chapter 4 is an expanded version of "The Civilizational, Spatial, and Sexual Powers of the Secular," published in *Varieties of Secularism in a Secular Age*, edited by Michael Warner, Jonathan Vanantwerpen, and Craig Calhoun (Harvard University Press, 2010). Chapter 5 is an updated version of "Gendered Nature of the Public Sphere," published in *Public Culture* 10, no. 1 (1997). Chapter 6 was initially published in *Public Culture* 14, no. 1 (2002). Chapter 7 was first published in *Cultural Politics* 5, no. 3 (2009). And chapter 8 is based on an earlier version of "Europe's Encounter with Islam: What Future?" published in *Constellations* 13, no. 2 (2006).

I express my gratitude to Zehra Cunillera, my PhD student at EHESS, assistant and team member of my EuroPublicIslam Project, who contributed to the editorial preparation, updating the empirical data as well as bibliographical sources.

1 Public Sphere beyond Religious-Secular Dichotomies

We live in a time when the religious/secular divide is being transformed. This book considers this process from the perspective of several national and cultural contexts in which Islamic revivals have been a major factor. In European countries, Muslim migrants have pressed their claim to religious visibility and thus have contested the secular norms of public life. In Turkey—a Muslim majority country with a tradition of strong secularism—the coming to power of the AKP, a party with an Islamic lineage, weakened the hegemony of secular elites. Both Muslim majority countries and European countries with Muslim migrant populations provide an empirical ground to examine the unsettling of the separation of powers between religion and the secular. The case studies in this book illustrate the ways these religious claims do not lead to a totalistic rejection of the secular but give way to new cultural constellations, re-assemblages, and realignments between secular and Muslim actors.

In contrast to those who see the "return of religion" as alternating with and replacing the power of the secular, this book depicts the dynamics in which both Islamic revival and secular modernity are acquiring new kinds of mutual framing. In that respect, Jürgen Habermas's "postsecular" thesis is a notable attempt to include the religious dimension in the readings of Western modernity. He deploys the term *postsecular* to mark and address the issue of religion in a secular society. He emphasizes the necessity of reflexivity that would alter both religious and secular mentalities and hence would contribute to the "modernization of public consciousness." According to him "the public consciousness of postsecular society reflects a normative insight that has consequences for how believing and unbelieving citizens interact with one another politically."[1]

Scholars working on case studies from both western and nonwestern contexts have sought to complicate and extend the notion of the postsecular.[2] They question Habermas's emphasis on the neutrality of public reason. They contend that religious traditions can be differentially articulated to the modern condition and its accompanying "immanent frame"[3] by mobilizing the language and the imaginary of a given religion. Thus religion functions not only as a source of normative meaning but also as a form of social criticism. By attending to the importance of (and hunger for) the sacred in a disenchanted world, religions raise and give voice to new concerns about life under modern conditions. Postsecular society is not a desecularized society, but a society where religious and secular views are called to live together. The copresence within the same public sphere of religious and secular worldviews and practices points to a steady weakening of the rigid borders between the two. A lived proximity of differences, accentuated by public confrontations and controversies, leads to a process of "interpenetration" between worldviews and practices.[4] These confrontational and dialectical interactions also reshape the dividing lines and open up the possibility of new configurations of both the secular and the religious.

The same processes show us that we need some critical distance from the paradigm of Eurocentric narratives of modernity and some "opening up of the social sciences."[5] It is necessary to revise the taken-for-granted Euroamerican sociological presuppositions in a world in which the distinctions between the east and the west, the Islamic and the modern, secular are no longer empirically plausible, where the established boundaries are continuously shifting. Only by rejecting the universalistic assumption that Western experience provides both normative and sociohistoric yardsticks for measuring the compliance of societies with modernity, we can open up our readings to nonwestern "habitations" of modernity.[6] Actors of Islam are critically appropriating and reinventing the modern experience. It is at the level of microsociological everyday life practices of social actors, as embodied in grammars of sexuality and intimacy and as expressed in the use of space, that we can trace the elaborations of religious and secular norms in the public making. The notions of "local," "multiple," and "alternative" modernities enable us to deconstruct the secular Western narratives, and especially to highlight novel and creative forms of publicness.[7]

We need to acknowledge that there is not one "ideal model" of secularism—whether it is defined by the Anglo-Saxon liberalism, stressing religious freedom; or by the French republican "laïcité," imposing emancipation from religion as a condition of modernity. It is possible to identify different genealogies of the secular, its cultural interpretations and habitations in the nonwestern contexts. Turkey and India provide two compelling cases of alternative formations of the secular: Turkish secularism is the product of a nation-building process, whereas Indian secularism emerged in the course of decolonization. In Turkey, secularism became the vector of westernization and homogenization of a national culture that marked the transition from a multireligious, multiethnic Ottoman Empire. In India, secularism was adopted to obviate religious strife between Hindus and Muslims in a new independent republic. There are many secularisms following different historical trajectories and acquiring new meanings.

In nonwestern historical contexts, secularism signals a wide range of cultural meanings and political commitments. Secularism here also has a broader scope of applications, well beyond the requisite separation of state and religion. It facilitates the formation of secular elites, promotes their vision of modernity, and valorizes their westernized lifestyle. Kemalism in Turkey is considered to be the most elaborate form of vernacular secularism in a Muslim society. Not simply an authoritarian secularism from above instituted to exclude religion from the affairs of the state, Kemalism aggressively sought to reorganize Turkish society according to secular rules, principles, and laws, retaining Islam as a cultural presence. As in the case of French secularism, Turkish secularism is not totally free of religion. Just as French laïcité holds a particular articulation with Christianity and represents a form of "catho-laïcité," Turkish *laiklik* also displays some characteristics of Islam. It pretends to be neutral, yet it tacitly endorses Sunnite-majority norms. As is so often the case, secularity has developed in a way that intertwines it with the particular religion from which it attempts to distance itself. The contest between the religious and the secular implicates different fields, ranging from the formation of the state, to the dynamics of the public sphere, to the ethics of self. The debate around the Islamic headscarf of Muslim women in public schools and universities—a debate that polarized the societies of both France and Turkey—is the most telling example of the confrontation between Islamic and secular values. The headscarf issue reveals the battleground on all these three levels: governance, public visibility of religious signs, and private pious self.

The intensification of Islamic movements from the 1980s onward has given rise to a wide range of new Muslim subjectivities in large part through the public display of intimate, sacred, and pious values and practices. The adoption of Islamic modes of covering in public places, especially in schools, universities, Parliament, hospitals, swimming pools, and sports competitions, has often defied secular norms underpinning those spaces and activities. The result has been disorienting, both to the individuals who find such spaces changing around them and to the established power relations that manifest themselves in public norms. The separation of the tacit and the visible, the secular and the religious, no longer holds in the same form, as enhanced Islamic visibility has engendered transgressions, confrontations, and mutual transformations.

In the contexts covered here, national public spheres that once were comparatively homogeneous now include new Muslim visibilities and imaginaries. The actors of "second wave" Islamism increasingly blend into modern urban spaces, engage in public debates, adopt consumption patterns, and organize their everyday life in secular time. They increasingly engage their faith reflexively amid a multitude of everyday secular practices. They draw on both secular and religious idioms to fashion their place in public life and help cultivate common norms for living together.

6

During the last three decades, we have witnessed the ways in which the visibility of Islamic signs and symbols in European public life has become a major source of cultural dissonance and political dispute. Islam has turned from a *longue durée* theological and macro entity into a present-day controversial issue in European public life. No longer confined to the private domain, Islam has gone public and has become hypervisible. This public staging of Islam in European democracies has triggered a sustained debate about the presence of Muslims and the challenge they pose to the taken-for-granted cultural values of Europe. In the course of these debates, the values that govern the public order—namely secularism, freedom of expression, and tolerance, as well as values concerning the private or personal sphere, such as women's status—come to the forefront.

Muslim actors manifest their religious difference by means of symbols, signs, and performances. Their "visibility" or becoming visible is a constitutive part of Islamic agency. Islamic imaginaries are in many ways carried by images rather than by ideologies. Women's veils, minarets and mosques, and halal dietary habits thus can be taken as master symbols of Islam. These religious symbols and practices in public life contribute to the production of a collective Muslim imaginary that circulates among different publics, irrespective of differences in national language communities.

Controversies around Islam have increasingly placed the aesthetic realm under public scrutiny. The domains of visual art, literature, architecture, and fashion have increasingly become invested with Islamic representations. Sacred symbols of Islam have been represented, albeit by satire and condescension, in genres as different as Salman Rushdie's novel *Satanic Verses* and the Danish cartoons of Muhammad. The artistic domain has often refracted public controversies around Islam, capturing the battle between secular norms of freedom and the sacred prohibitions of Islam. The social worlds of art have also provided interactive spaces for cultures and publics otherwise foreign to each other. Art has in many ways contributed to new bonds between different citizen groups—not without elements of confrontation, mutual rejection, and violence. Despite the discord and the controversies, one can observe that Islam is in the process of becoming an indigenous reference, the "familiar other" for the European publics.

The public sphere provides a stage for bringing together and reassembling citizens of different cultural and social backgrounds, including both migrants and natives. The public sphere is linked to the democratic experience of pluralism to the extent that it is not exclusively monitored by state power—a place of national consensus and juridical regulation—but remains open to newcomers and to their manifestation of difference. A recognition of dissensus and of antagonism enables one to apprehend the public sphere as a space for exploration of norms and ways of living together. It is not static. It is continuously re-created anew and inhabited by diverse actors who manifest and confront their differences in verbal and corporeal practices. The public sphere is not solely a receptacle to which newcomers must conform themselves in order to gain access; it also provides a democratic site where newcomers can argue over their places and their norms. The public sphere is the site for confrontational proximity and copenetration. The appearance of *différend*[8] is characteristic of a democratic public sphere and is not symptomatic of its dysfunction. Indeed, an agonistic notion of the public space allows us to approach it as a site to which social actors try to gain access in order to manifest their difference and dispute the majority's norms for collective life. From this perspective, the notion of controversy becomes a privileged methodological tool for studying discord that simultaneously confronts and binds different actors together.[9] A focus on controversy and an agonistic approach to the public sphere are therefore necessary for understanding the changing relations between the secular and the religious. In this sense, placing the notion of the public sphere at the center of our analysis enables us to study the dynamics of encounters and confrontation, leading us to question the interface between private and public, personal and intercultural.

In the last two or three decades, the controversies around

Islamic religious symbols and norms have provoked more fear and anxiety than mutual recognition. Islamic visibility and difference have had a disruptive effect in different European publics, showing the difficulties of accommodating Islam in terms of minority rights. The established normative frames of cultural pluralism, religious freedom, or individual liberties were often abandoned in response; in much dominant rhetoric Islam is externalized as an "alterité," an incommensurable monolithic reality against which Europeans try to distinguish and protect themselves. With the announcement of the end of multiculturalism and the critiques of cultural relativism, European politics began to drift toward the defense of national identity, the superiority of European cultural values, and the exceptionalism of Western civilization. The increasing popularity of far-right parties and neopopulist movements—who put on top of their agenda the fight against the "invasion of Islam" and euro-skepticism—points to the shortfalls of European democracies.

Islam appears as the unexpected, the blind spot, *l'impensé* of the European political project. In Francis Fukuyama's widely discussed thesis, the fall of the Berlin Wall signaled the end of conflict with communism and marked the end of history.[10] The intellectuals of Eastern and Central Europe, in contrast to the Western narrative of the end of history, saw this as an opportunity, a "rebirth of history."[11] The expansion of the frontiers of the European Union toward the East revived the notion of Mitteleuropa. A new "post-western" dimension of Europe was coming into play, entailing a "general decline of the West as the overarching reference point for Europe." This new focus on East-

Central Europe brought into the debates the imperial legacies of the Russian, Ottoman, and Habsburg Empires. As a consequence, it is increasingly difficult to define European civilization in terms of a unitary notion of modern Western civilization.

Gerard Delanty speaks of three concentric heritages of European civilization. On his account, not only the Christian West, but also the Slavic Byzantine and the Muslim Ottoman Empire are constitutive elements of the history of Europe. With the fall of the Berlin Wall, Eastern Europe has once again come into prominence, and there is a growing recognition of the Orthodox Russian historic heritage in the making of Europe. However, the Ottoman heritage is still usually left outside.[12] Even the extensive debate over Turkey's EU candidacy has not led to a reconsideration and appreciation of that heritage. On the contrary, the hostility against the candidacy of Turkey can be read as an indication that the historic influence of Ottoman Islam inside Europe is being systematically denied, if not erased.

Internal Muslim differences are also playing a decisive role in the redefinition of European identity. According to Andre Gingrich, a new kind of Orientalism—"frontier orientalism"—maintains a distinction between two kinds of the Oriental, the good Bosnian one and the bad Turkish one. Frontier orientalism aims at "overcoming the Bad Muslim" for identity building, "while relying on a controlled Good Muslim."[13] However, even the indigenous good Muslims do not fare all that well in drawing the boundaries of the so-called new Europe. The ethnic cleansing directed against Muslim and Croat populations in Bosnia during the 1992–1995 war testifies to the tragic consequences of frontier orientalism.

The Turkish EU candidacy played a cathartic role in uncovering the malaise and anxiety surrounding the question of European identity. The distancing and othering of Turkey drew the boundaries of Europe in religious and civilizational terms. Europe came to be defined by fixed geographical borders, historical heritage, and cultural values. Turkey as a Muslim-majority candidate for the EU and a Muslim-migrant country crystallized in different ways the "absent-presence" of Muslims in Europe, both from within and outside Europe. Some feared Islamic invasion and considered Turkish membership as a "Trojan horse" that would carry Islam into Christian lands; some criticized political elites who imposed Turkey as a "forced marriage" and defended popular sovereignty of Europe; others saw Europe as defined by the conservation of historical memories and feared that Turkish membership in the Union would mean renouncing the victory of Europe over the Ottoman Empire in 1683 at the gates of Vienna. In general, the admission of Turkey would mean weakening European identity and extending its frontiers toward the dangerous East.

A second move toward redefining European identity can be located in regard to the debates over its Christian roots. A tacit equation between Europe and Christianity has been expressed more and more overtly in recent public debates. Pope Benedict XVI, in his widely quoted speech at Regensburg in 2006, argued that Christianity, contrary to Islam, is a religion of reason; he urged European intellectuals not to dismiss Christian spiritual sources in defining European identity and tolerance. Whether or not there should be a reference to Christian values in the European Constitution was, at the time, the subject of intense debate among the member countries of Europe, until the leadership of France blocked it.

These examples enable us to notice and track the changing self-presentation of Europeans in their encounters with different facets of Islam. European self-presentation often turns to and draws on its civilizational roots, but defining Europe as a civilization shifts the defense, in ways that are often unnoticed, from Europe's claim to universality—as explicitly enunciated in Enlightenment pedagogy—toward an insistence on distinctiveness and European exceptionalism. In other words, European historical experience, once proposed as the universal model of modernity and offered as an example for emulation by non-Western people, is undergoing a severe ideological contraction motivated by a drive to preserve its alleged purity and distinction. Immigration and the increasing manifestation of Islam in Europe have given rise to an inward-looking politics of identity, stressing the need for securing national boundaries against the flood of threatening signs and images of difference. These new dynamics of closure not only risk damaging democratic pluralism but also work against the ideals of European union, which envision a pluralism beyond nationalism.

Turkey: Torn between Civilizations or Culturally Crossbred?

Turkey can be taken as a laboratory where the prospects of surpassing the divide or risking a violent clash are both equally present.[14] Samuel Huntington's controversial thesis regarding the clash of civilizations has reinjected the notion of civilization in the public/academic discourse on foreign policy and international relations. According to Huntington, whereas the main lines of conflict during the Cold War were primarily political and derived their explosive nature from considerations of national interest and international security, the lines of fracture today correspond to major cultural antagonisms involving a clash of values between civilizations. As for the specific conflict between the Western and Islamic civilizations, he suggests that it "has been going on for 1,300 years" and is destined to continue, with periodic violent eruptions, because these religious-cultural differences, unlike political differences, are incommensurable.[15] The culture, identity, and religious faith that used to be subordinated to political and military strategy now define priorities on the international political agenda. We are witnessing the invasion of politics by culture. Divisions between civilizations are becoming threats to international stability and world order.

According to Huntington, Turkey represents a torn country, and her attempt to integrate with the Western world by adopting its values and joining its institutions can never be attained. The fact that its population is predominantly Muslim makes it impossible to treat Turkey as an equal member of the West. On the other hand, the Islamic world does not see Turkey as being Muslim enough. Turkey's close ties with the West and her devotion to secularism raise suspicion and resentment. To overcome this torn condition, Huntington recommends that Turkey should abandon her ambitions to Westernize and, instead, play for the leadership of the Islamic world. In short, Turkey should give up Atatürk's secular legacy and affiliate herself with the Arab world in order to lead it and perhaps fulfill her civilizational destiny.[16]

Alternatively, one might view Turkey not as a "torn country" caught in the opposed gravitational pull of two civilizations, but as a hybrid country representing a "mode of non-western postsecular modernity," capable of constructively mediating between Islam and the West, between the religious and the secular. With the AKP coming to power, the Kemalist mode of assertive secularism that sought to suppress the presence of religion has lost its grip over public life and is being replaced by what one might call "passive secularism."[17] Assertive secularism was the dominant ideology in the founding of the Turkish Republic whose golden era was the period from 1933 to 1949, when there was not a single legal school or university teaching Islam. The passive secularists, from Turgut Özal (1927–1993) to Tayyib Erdogan, have interpreted secularism as a characteristic of the state, not of individuals, and have recognized that religion has sociocultural ramifications beyond an individual's conscience. Recently, Erdogan declared that he could view himself as "a secular individual" in upholding the secular characteristic of the state, while eschewing the Kemalist secularism geared to colonize every aspect of everyday life. Massimo Rosati suggests that Turkey is not simply shifting from an assertive to a passive conception of secularism but becoming, at least sociologically speaking, a laboratory for a postsecular society.[18] Indeed the coexistence of the AKP with a secular state, involving complementary learning processes between religious and secular actors, has transformed Turkish political life during the 2000s. Hybrid political actors—conservative democrats, Muslim intellectuals, pious bourgeoisie, and female public personages—attest to a deepening of democratic experience.

Whether Turkey represents a model for surpassing the

religious-secular divide, or on the contrary risks becoming a "torn country" in which different civilizational alignments drift away, remains an open-ended question.

Public Space, Pluralism, and Religious/Secular Realignments

The public sphere serves as the privileged site for testing the existence of a pluralistic democracy in a postsecular society. The exclusion of religious signs by a secular state or the imposition of religious morality in public by an Islamic state undermines the exploratory potential of the public sphere.

The Gezi Park movement in Istanbul is an illustrative case in point, but the significance of public square movements in opening new avenues for democratic imaginaries is not limited to Turkey. From the Arab world to the western capitals, from Turkey to Ukraine, a wave of protest movements—different as they are—has injected new democratic energies and agendas into the public square. They attest to the importance of publicness, the politics of space, and the roles of art, humor, and performance in enacting pluralism.

The protestors converge around claims for dignity, commitment to justice, and practices of pluralism. Rather than trying to overcome their differences, to efface them in the name of collective identities, these public space movements celebrate plurality. They recognize and acknowledge each other's differences and explore together the possibilities for forging new bonds. These movements are different from the organized political movements of the past—leftist, nationalist, and Islamist—as they lack a core ideology and leadership. They are also different from the identity movements of the 1980s, such as feminism. Yet they generate a sense of solidarity, a sense of enchantment of togetherness and civic resistance. They defy political authoritarianism and reject neoliberal capitalism. They bring the micropolitics of everyday life into the realm of democracy.

An urban development project designed to build a shopping mall in place of Gezi Park, a public garden in the midst of Taksim Square in Istanbul, triggered an environmentalist movement of resistance in May 2013. With the disproportionate use of brute force by the riot police, especially their massive use of tear gas, the movement achieved a new momentum and gained overwhelming support of the middle classes, spreading from Istanbul to all other cities in Turkey. Perhaps because it lacked a central ideology or leadership, it quickly gained a national following turned into a public forum to express the growing discontent and frustrations with the AKP government.

The Gezi Park movement bore characteristics of both Middle Eastern and Western social protest movements. We can find elements from the Tahrir Square movement in Egypt as well as from the "indignados" in European cities or Occupy Wall Street in the United States. The Gezi Park movement was also similar to European activists protesting against global economic forces. In other ways the Turkish debate was and remains specific. While European activists such as the indignados (the "outraged," defending their dignity against neoliberalism) were reacting to threats posed by economic instability, the Turkish protesters were criticizing hyperdevelopment. The anticapitalist tone of the Gezi Park protest movement challenged the governing political power because of its Islamic affiliation. With the

AKP in power, Islam ceased to be an idiom of the urban poor, the politically excluded classes, and became a medium of empowerment for both the state apparatus and the new, affluent middle classes. Turkey with its economic success story represented an emerging power in the region. In that respect, the Gezi protestors were similar to Brazilians, who also profited from a decade of rapid economic growth and yet expressed outrage at grandiose urban projects linked to the 2014 FIFA World Cup and the 2016 Rio Olympics.

The Gezi Park movement also resembles the occupation of Tahrir Square that gave voice to the long suffering and deep anger of the Egyptian people against an authoritarian regime. However, the political contexts are dissimilar. The Arab Spring was about the dissolution of an authoritarian regime and the occupation of the public space, the Maydan al-Tahrir, and expressed the demand of the majority to have a voice via democratic elections. The Gezi movement is not about changing or overthrowing the government but about defending minority voices that have been disregarded in the context of a majoritarian concept of electoral democracy. Defending a few trees in Istanbul's Gezi Park against the plans to build a glittering shopping mall unexpectedly became a tipping point marking a dramatic shift in political alignments and the accompanying manifestation of a new critical consciousness. For the inhabitants of Istanbul, the project of constructing a shopping mall in the middle of Gezi Park meant private capital's confiscation of public space, the enclosure of the commons.

In the Gezi Park movement, environmental sensitivities and the critique of global capitalism became intertwined. In general, capitalism tends to manifest itself through abstract forces, like globalization, financial markets, and neoliberalism, and thus escapes the grip of politics. In Turkey, however, capitalism as materially incarnated in the shopping mall was a new and concrete symbol of global financial capitalism. The initial enthusiasm for malls as convenient places for shopping as well as for social gatherings quickly faded and gave rise to a new concern about how untrammelled greed and consumerism boosted by Islamic power were severely undermining the already fragile urban fabric. The spectacular growth of the Turkish economy under the AKP government has been widely acknowledged. However, this success story was also subjected to criticism, including among Muslims. A Muslim youth movement drawing its support from anticapitalist Muslims had already articulated its criticisms of "pious capitalism" and hyperdevelopment prior to the Gezi Park movement, which it has since joined.

The Gezi Park movement had a pluralistic democratic agenda. Its opposition to the construction of urban mega projects promoted by profit-seeking private capital was brought into focus around the shrinking of shared public spaces. At the same time, the Gezi Park protestors criticized and resisted the muzzling of public discourse and media by the government.

The Gezi Park movement also included, rather prominently, the so-called anxious secular moderns. From the very beginning of AKP's ascension to power, this group had been concerned about the potential constriction of secular ways of life and intrusions into private spaces by the government. This concern sometimes verges on Islamophobia and nostalgia for the previous military regime, prompting "demonstrations for the defense of the Republic" (2007 Cumhuriyet Mitingleri). The decree regulating the sale of alcohol in early 2013 and moralistic rhetoric deployed to justify the decree had further deepened the suspicion that public life was being increasingly regimented in conformity with Islamic values. The anxious secular moderns, angered and alienated, mobilized to defend their way of life prior to the Gezi Park movement.

Although the presence of a new generation of anxious secular moderns was palpable, if not dominant in the Gezi Park movement, their attitude—unlike their parents'—was free of intolerance toward their fellow Muslim protesters. This is a clear indication that Gezi Park is one among many public spaces where the Turkish version of secularism is being historically transformed. In the process, the rhetoric of the secular is being de-linked from the state ideological apparatus and realigned with the micropolitics of the *meydan*, the public square.

The meydan (public space in Turkish, which evokes a circle rather than a square; a cognate of *maidan*) furnished a stage for political actors of various persuasions to interact creatively and perform together. The Gezi Park movement realigned people across old divisions and enmities. It gave rise to new forms of citizenship practices prompted by the unexpected and creative assemblages and encounters of people in the meydan. Many of these encounters involved public performances and personal agency—whirling dervishes, public praying in the park, and making the common meal for breaking the Ramadan fast. The performance of one whirling dervish at the meydan is a particularly instructive measure of the new religious/secular interinvolvement. Ziya Azazi, an Austrian performance artist of Turkish origin, whirled wearing a tear gas mask in his dervish costume. He connected the traditional Sufi spiritual performance with the symbol of resistance, the gas mask. Photographs and videos of the performance were quickly disseminated via the Internet. The whirling dervish thus became one of the most captivating images of the Gezi Park movement.

The respect accorded to Islamic rituals and observant Muslims by the secular protestors was a compelling indicator that something new was afoot at Gezi Park. The traditional antagonisms were giving way to a new spirit of understanding and cooperation. In a moving scene, while a group of observant Muslims performed their Friday prayer in the park and under rain, other protestors, including members of the young atheist association, held umbrellas over them. Another exemplary case occurred on the sacred day of Miraj, Prophet Muhammad's heavenly ascension. Gezi Park protestors passed out special patisserie *kandil simidi* (sesame bagels) made for this occasion. On that religious holiday a poster with the following proclamation was posted all over the park: "No to alcohol, no fighting, no bad words, no provocation, and no violence. Yes to respect, peace, prayer, protest and kandil simidi." The poster also featured an image of the sacred sesame bagel with the hippie peace sign next to it, signifying the emergence of a new alliance by crossing symbols from two hitherto opposed idioms.

This display of camaraderie across the religious/secular divide culminated in the festive organization of a collective fast-breaking dinner, *iftar*, during Ramadan. These meals, called "mother earth meals" (*yeryüzü sofrası*), were organized on the initiative of anticapitalist Muslims. In the presence of secular youth—ranging from liberals to communists, Kemalists to gay activists—the Muslim organizers issued a blistering attack against the AKP government. They criticized AKP's often used strategy of promoting and implementing capitalist ventures detrimental to the public good under the cover of Islamist rhetoric, while systematically marginalizing, if not abandoning, the religious values and commitments of the common people. The contrast between the official celebration of iftar and its Gezi Park counterpart was inescapable. While the municipalities set their sumptuous separate tables in glittering five-star hotels, the Gezi Park protesters set a single 650-meter-long table on Istiklal Street in Beyoglu, in front of the famous Francophone Lycée de Galatasaray. People brought their own meal and shared it with others in the streets at this long table. The mingling of the "cool" secular youth and the "pious" anticapitalist Muslim youth at the public meals created an atmosphere of communion under which the politics of secular/religious polarization seemed obsolete. For a moment at that long table, the deep-seated suspicion and hostility between the two Turkeys had evaporated and the country was "torn" no more.

Public space democracy provides a potential for relinquishing the political polarizations, cultural hierarchies, and civilizational alterity between the religious and the secular, between the traditional and the modern. It is at the phenomenological level, at the level of microsociological everyday practices, that one can observe the transformative potential of the public sphere. First, in light of worldwide public space movements, the West ceases to be the sole source of democratic inspiration and innovation. As Islamic societies struggle to find new ways of coarticulating faith and pluralism, they are rejecting the vicious circle of alternating between secular authoritarianism and political Islam. The protest movements in both Turkey and the Arab world have not only unsettled the secular/religious divide but also paved new convergences between the Islamic societies and the West. In their respective efforts to integrate Islam within democratic polity, they are learning from each other's success or failure. A mimetic reversal is occurring between the West and the East. Now that the West is no longer the only standard bearer of democracy, interconnected imaginaries and transverse solidarities between different societies are emerging. As Jeffrey Alexander rightly points out, "there is an unprecedented connection of Eastern and Western impulses, demonstrating that the tide of democratic thought and action is hardly confined to Judeo-Christian civilizations."[19] He argues that the social upheavals in both the West and the East should be read within the same "narrative arc."

Second, public space movements have become a site for new forms and norms of public-making among actors with different habitus and belief systems. While mingling in these spaces, they explore new modes of interaction, collaboration, and habitation. In that process, an anonymous collective energy (not unlike Durkheim's "effervescence" but often sustained through a sense of crisis) is released, and a new repertoire of political actions—performative and artistic—become visible. Such is the pedagogy of the meydan.

These movements draw attention to the importance of spatiality in the practice of pluralism. As evident from the public gatherings at Tahrir Square, Gezi Park, Wall Street, the Maidan in Kiev, and other places, the physicality of space is crucial for manifesting a plurality of differences while pursuing a common cause and for staging protests against authoritarian regimes. These places—meydans, public squares, parks, and streets—provide, as in a theater, a stage on which different actors can display their ideals and aspirations, personally and publicly.

Third, democratic majoritarianism as a taken-for-granted political norm is creatively challenged at the meydan. Here one may observe the interplay between two distinct and competing ways of practicing democracy, namely institutional/electoral politics and the public sphere. The political puts forth the representative nature of democracy and the collective will of the nation, whereas the public incites in the present the experience of pluralism as a "happening." Public space democracy provides a stage for "active minorities"—those who do not comply with the established majority norms of public life and collective identity—to manifest their differences freely. They illustrate that minorities are not only preestablished entities coinciding with certain religious or ethnic groups, but are also always in the process of becoming.

One of the main characteristics of public life in modern society is what Michael Warner calls "stranger sociability."[20] Worldwide public meydan movements can be read as a staged form of stranger sociability. They reassemble people who discover and cherish a mode of sociability and solidarity among those who do not share the same habitus and worldview. Social actors participating in meydan movements are not primarily motivated by identitarian concerns. They seek and enact commonness across identity groups without erasing differences; they innovate and perform collectively new forms of citizenship in an inclusionary fashion.

Religious Contestations of European Modernity

Social mobility and the circulation of ideas bring together actors with different and potentially conflicting cultural norms and attachments under the same nation-state. These social actors, deeply shaped by the forces associated with globalization, still adhere to the boundaries of a national community and a nation-state. Multiculturalism and cosmopolitanism, the two dominant modes of organizing differences, are clearly embedded within national and/or secular imaginaries. For that reason, they do not fully capture and resonate with the question of religious differences and civilizational divides in contemporary societies. Stranger sociability is no longer just a desired feature of modernity; it is also a source of social anxiety. The flaneur, the emblematic figure of modern cities, has given way to the *migrant* of the suburb. Stranger enmity, the politics of fear, and the use of hate discourse and violence in public life have become major concerns for democracies. The emerging nationalist and neopopulist movements that propagate Islamophobia, along with new forms of anti-Semitism among Islamist groups, damage profoundly the possibility of public-making. Furthermore, the tendency of the political powers to monitor the public sphere, to impose public order and sustain security by means of regulation and legislation, undercuts the democratic potential for a participatory public sphere. The historical context in which we are living in Europe illustrates the difficulty of rethinking the relation between the religious and the political Islam in the West.

The European intellectual legacy is itself shaped by critiques of Western modernity. The antimodernist tradition is an intrinsic part of modernity.[21] But critiques of modernity are not limited to Western thinking. The impact of the West on different historical and cultural contexts, the experiences of colonialism, the interdependence between the center and the periphery, varieties of diasporic histories, have determined in different ways the language of criticism in the human sciences. A plethora of critical schools and traditions—critiques of "Orientalism," Indian postcolonial studies, the historiography of the subaltern, Latin American dependence theory, and more recently the multiple/alternative modernities thesis—have deeply transformed the Eurocentric and standardized ways of narrating modernity. However, these powerful critiques of European modernity and predatory capitalism do not adequately capture the nature of Islamic discord with secular modernity. These theories were conceived in relation to a historical context in which geographical remoteness, differences in historical temporality, and *longue durée* structures mattered. In the present context, with the erasing of temporal and spatial boundaries, Islam becomes a contemporary of the West and resides within Europe as a neighbor among neighbors.

In that respect Europe provides, more than any other place, a privileged site to observe the ways in which the differential attitudes toward modernity become a battleground between religious and secular agents. Islamic discourse speaks from a vantage point that is thought to be external to the Western En-lightenment tradition. But at the same time, Islam becomes a source of reference and political contestation for those Muslims who are already de-territorialized, adulterated, and situated within the life experiences of European modernity. The signifi-cance of contemporary Islam rises from this double conversa-tion and binding between modernity and religion. Religious agencies question and critique such cultural forms and norms of modernity as liberal definitions of self, gender equality, pri-vate/public boundaries, and secularism. Hence a new reper-toire of conflicts arises, ranging from the conceptions of self, gender, and daily morality to the overall legitimacy of the polity. Thus Islam functions as an alternative ideological resource to dispute the cultural orientations of modernity. However, this disputation occurs within rather than outside the folds of modernity, because its Muslim disputants are already impli-cated in the spaces, experiences, temporalities, and media cul-ture of modernity. In other words, Islam, far from remaining un-altered as a distinct civilization, enters into the world-making scene and becomes part of the space of the modern through Muslim agencies. In turn, it challenges the Western claims of civilizational ownership of modernity.

The impact of Western European modernity on Muslim minds and societies is not a recent phenomenon. It has a long and checkered history. Various political projects and social processes such as colonialism, the civilizing mission, volun-tary westernization, authoritarian secularism, and waves of immigration have decisively shaped Muslim societies in their encounter with European modernity. In that encounter, still unfolding, Muslims have selectively appropriated some Western norms, institutions, and practices because of their universalist appeal, while rejecting others as parochial. On the whole, Muslims have been engaged in a prolonged conversation with Western modernity with shifting attitudes and moods ranging from subservience to anger, from Western mimicry to native authenticity. They have sought to measure and transform their polity and culture by drawing on and comparing with the hegemonic Western models. Historically, this has been largely an asymmetrical encounter and conversation. However, that has changed in the contemporary global context, especially in the case of Islam in Europe. Islam is no longer out there in Asia and elsewhere to be subdued and dominated. It is here in full visibility and demanding insistently its right to participate in and contribute to the making of a new Europe. As Islam and Western societies are getting into closer contact, in proximity with each other, and hence sharing the same European spaces and temporality, the nature of their relation is changing from a unilateral hegemonic domination to a reciprocal horizontal interaction. This interaction, despite the persistent asymmetrical power relations, has triggered a process of mutual transformation. Consequently, one can no longer grasp the fluid and evolving relations between Islam and the West in terms of geographical distance and temporal lag. Islam is now inside Europe, not elsewhere. It is a not very distant mirror in which Europe has sought to define and fashion herself in recent years. However, reading the European project in the mirror of Islam is not an easy task. Islam, in different ways, disrupts the public norms and unsettles the European self-understanding. While being inside Europe, Islam has become too visibly different due to sheer numbers and proximity. Moreover, Muslim agencies routinely use religious difference in their self-presentations in ways that strain European secular sensibilities—especially the capacity for tolerance. In this sense the Muslim presence in Europe becomes disturbing and gives rise to fear and resentment.

The presence of Islam has radically altered our ways of thinking about the prospect of secular modernity and the direction of European politics. This book adopts a dual perspective and endeavors to grasp the consequences of the historic unsettling of the religious/secular divide in Europe, Turkey, and elsewhere. As a sociologist, working and living in both Istanbul and Paris during the last twenty years, I have witnessed and examined a series of critical events in the history of two countries with strong secular traditions trying to grapple with a new group—hybrid Muslim actors—and the challenge they pose and embody. Being myself a product of two strong republican state traditions, French and Turkish, I had to understand, both as a person and as a sociologist, the religious challenges to the secular narrative. As a woman of a secular and feminist background, the Islamic headscarf controversy crystallized for me the (im)possible encounter with Islam. The controversies around the Turkish EU candidacy presented a second nodal point of encounter between Europe and Islam in which I was personally implicated.

This book expresses my intellectual concern to understand Islam as the inconceivable element of secular Western modernity. For me, the practice of sociology requires the adoption of a double cultural gaze, but it also entails a double distancing in order to translate the incommensurable cultural differences to one another. That is why I have privileged the site of the public sphere to study the ongoing cultural drama with a potential to open up a new horizon for the creation of a new choreography, a new common script.

The academic discipline of sociology, which has shaped the comprehension of modernity as an intrinsically secular process of change, faces today new challenges raised by the revival of religion in general and of Islam in particular. European sociology confronts these challenges in a more significant and dramatic way to the extent that Europe becomes a site where particular modes of encounter between the principles of secular modernity and Muslim religious claims are taking place at the level of everyday life practices and are debated in different national publics. In the last three decades, by means of religious claims of Muslim migrants and new controversies in the public life, Islam, an external reference, is becoming an indigenous one in European public life. We can speak of the reterritorialization of Islam in Europe, its "Europeanization" and indigenization, which, however, does not follow a dynamics of assimilation in conformity with European secular modernity. In other words, Islam is becoming contemporary with Europe both in terms of proximity in time and in space but in confrontation with the principles of European secular modernity. Islam competes with the European *chronotope*, the European narrative of time and space.[1] The Bakhtinian notion of chronotope indicates variety of presents embedded in different spaces and therefore suggests a way to explore beyond the secular modernity.

"De-centering" European sociology or displacing the sociological gaze with an anthropological sensibility for difference in non-Western territories and cultural habitations of modernity helped to engage a critical stand in social sciences.[2] But the present forms of encounter between Islam and Europe take place in the same chronotope (correlation between time and space) without the geographical distance and time lag between the Western colonizer and the colonized, between the modern European and the traditional Muslims, which in turn necessitate framing the relation in terms of transnational and intercultural (read intercivilizational) terms. Consequently, the intimate encounters between Islam and Europe engender a mutual transformation that calls for a two-way mirroring and intercultural reflexivity, only possible by means of liberating European narratives of modernity—and sociology—from their colonial frame and universalist claim.

Over the last two decades, the studies on Islam started to occupy a central place on the social science agenda. Such a resurgence of interest in Islam is related to the revival of religious claims and movements that have transformed the political and public scene in Muslim-majority countries as well as in Western contexts. The use of Islam as a reference for the self-presentation by diverse social groups such as youth, women, and migrants in the contemporary world poses a challenge to the Western narratives of secular modernity. With the emergence of contemporary forms of Islam that range from the Iranian Revolution and women's veiling to jihadist movements, studies on Islam cease to be a field reserved exclusively to Orientalists, theologians, or area studies specialists and move to the center of the research agenda of political sciences, sociology, anthropology, and law. Increasingly, interdisciplinary approaches are used to study contemporary forms of Islamic religiosity and agency. The entry of Islam on the research agenda brings forth new horizons of critique in social scientific agendas. We can speak of a new configuration of Islamic studies that unsettles the disciplinary frontiers and opens up critical readings of European modernity and sociology from the vantage point of Islam.

Can Islamic studies introduce the vantage point of the "subaltern" Muslim and decolonize European sociology? Can universalist claims of European sociology give way to new modes of articulating secularity and modernity and thereby contribute to the "opening of the social sciences"?[3] These are some of the novel questions that need to be addressed. Indeed, Islamic studies increasingly expand to different disciplines and transform their research agendas. I will evoke three major, broad, and cutting-edge research topics, namely, globalization, the public sphere, and gender, in order to elaborate on the ways Islam enters on these research agendas and in so doing unsettles the established frames of thought. I use the notion of Islam to the extent that Muslim actors in their present-day practices articulate their faith and agency in ways that challenge Western hegemony on definitions of modern global order, European public life, and gendered self.

The contemporary forms of Islam are studied and framed

differently depending on whether the emphasis is on religion, modes of governance, social norms and values, or modes of mobilization and confrontation. Different conceptualizations, such as religious revivalism, Islamic Sharia, cultural conservatism, terrorist-jihadist movements, and the "clash of civilizations," all designate the cross-disciplinary efforts to depict and comprehend the contours of contemporary Islam. However, the latter raise problems of conceptualization and labeling. Islamic studies have in fact attempted to name and conceptualize the imprint of Islam in the actions and interpretations of diverse actors. The notion of Islamism has had an advantage in establishing a distinction between Islam as a religion and its forms of political radicalization. The political science approaches to Islam have allowed us to understand contemporary forms of religious contestation that are not separable from the mobilization of masses, the seizure of state power, and the application of Sharia law. Nonetheless, political science approaches have a tendency to reduce the role of religion to its instrumentalization by groups of political power. Anthropological approaches, on the other hand, have underscored the importance of faith and studied the formations of religious subjectivities yet dissociated them from questions of agency and social problems. Sociological studies provided depictions of the role of urban groups, educated youth, women, and intellectuals in Islamic movements but remained within the limits of the state versus society dichotomy. The study of contemporary Islam calls for depicting the diversity of praxis and the transnational dynamics in which Islamic religion is reinterpreted and reactivated with the aim of shaping the intimate, public, and political lives of Muslims. Islamic movements do not merely target juridical governance and political life but equally affect the public and private spheres, that is to say, gender regimes, social morals, and spatial arrangements. The complexities of contemporary Islamic modes of expression and the new recompositions between faith and agency, secular and religious, personal and public, requires an interdisciplinary approach but furthermore a critique of the already established frames of Western sociological thought.

As sociological theories about secularization undergo a critical revision, the studies on the "return of religion" have gained a real interest. The two pillars on which the narrative of modernity was constructed, namely, secularization and the idea of progress, are challenged by the concomitant desire for the return of religion and for the forces of the immutable.[4] However, contemporary Islam is far from being a continuation of the chains of the historical past, and witnesses, on the contrary, a radical rupture and change. The imprint of the past, the religious and the traditional can only be captured within the prism of contemporary social forms of criticism and contestation. The Islamic movements are "rejuvenated" by the adherence of young and educated urban populations and "feminized" by the presence of girls and women who have begun to take on the veil since the 1980s (following a period of unveiling in the 1920s, in conformity with the secular reformist movements of elites in many Muslim countries such as Turkey, Iran, and Egypt). The revival of Islam means for many of its young and female followers a relearning of religious knowledge, studying the precepts, and rethinking the present issues from the prism of the religious past. The immutability promised by religion and the power of its longue durée history creates a veritable magnetism for those who seek guidance in a world governed by "presentism." According to Hartog, "presentism" is the consequence of the "collapse of the future" and of the linear, "progressive" time conception that has been underpinning national histories since the Enlightenment. Since the fall of the Berlin Wall, the contemporary regime of historicity privileges the present, not the past or the future, as the primary reference in time.[5] Islamic fundamentalism, however, revalorizes the link to the past. It draws on a model in the past, to the golden age of Islam rather than an unrealized ideal, a utopia. The text of the Quran and the life of the Prophet Muhammad serve as guidelines and sources of example for sorting out the grammar of leading a "truly" pious existence at the level of everyday life practices as well as for finding the right path in modern life.

Hence framing contemporary Islam as the "return of religion" reveals a more complex phenomenon than it appears. The notion of *religion* embodies and carries a plethora of meanings and praxis that require unpacking and criticism in the light of practices and interpretations of contemporary social actors. Islam(ism) is the name that refers to the conscious and collective ways of refashioning religion from the prism of contemporary issues in modern life politics and in a globalized world. In doing so, contemporary Islam enters on the historical stage of the present in debating and confronting the universalist claims of secular modernity and European social thinking. The entry of Islam into the realm of global politics, European publics, and sexual modernity unsettles the established power relations and frames of thought. The three realms correspond to three different scales on which Western modernity disputes its hegemony, namely the rules of the world order, the morals of the public life, and the sexual norms of the self. As I will elaborate more in chapter 3, these three realms and scales operate on different temporalities, but they exemplify the most central sites in tracking and debating the changes of Western European modernity. The social scientific agenda in general and sociology in particular search for understanding the new patterns of globalism and transnational dynamics, the cultural and religious difference in the public sphere, and the forms of sexual emancipation and feminism. Islamic studies enter these three pioneer areas and transform the intellectual agenda in challenging the definitions of transnational publics and self.

First, one has to be reminded that studies on globalization and Islam came to be related only recently, especially in the aftermath of 9–11. There is an increasing awareness that Islam cannot be studied within the confines of political dynamics in a given nation-state (as was the case with the Islamic revolution in Iran in 1979); neither can it be identified with one single region (such as the Middle East). It circulates among different publics, nations, and regions and becomes a global affair whether it is related to the phenomenon of immigration, to public controversies, or to terrorist acts. Second, Islam becomes public, meaning that religion, which is supposed to be contained within the private domain, claims visibility in the public arena. Third, questions of gender and sexuality are central in the course of contemporary Islamism but also in the process of confrontation with European publics. The Islamic veiling in public is a sign of transgressing spatial and gendered boundaries of the sacred private domain. Furthermore, staging the Islamic difference by means of the symbolism of the veil in the

European public spheres carries an ambivalent message: Muslim women claim their access and presence in the secular public life yet provoke a discord in unsettling the tacit rules and cultural codes of European public life.

The controversies on Islamic headscarves of Muslim students in French public schools or of teachers in Germany indicate clearly the way Islam ceases to be a Muslim-Muslim question and becomes a general concern for the European public.[6] Contemporary Islam provokes cultural malaise and mobilizes collective passion to the extent that the very foundations of secular modernity are thought to be threatened by the religious claims in public life. Islam is perceived as a threat to the most contemporary and highly valued achievements of European liberal democracies, such as sexual emancipation, gender equality, and freedom of expression. The public presence and staging of Islam in European democracies trigger a debate on the presence of Muslims in Europe, and well beyond that, on the cultural values of Europe. In the course of these debates, the values that govern the public order (secularism, freedom of expression, and tolerance) as well as the ones concerning the private or personal sphere (women's status, religious faith) come to be confronted with one another and then renegotiated, bringing about a displacement of boundaries between public and private, secular and religious, and Europe and Islam.

Islam on the Global Scene

The process of globalization brings people and cultures in closer contact. The anthropological distance and the frontiers between the self and the others, between the moderns and the indigenous, between the colonizers and the colonized are blurred, if not erased, within an increasingly interconnected globe. The reduction of time and space between different parts of the world brings together cultures, countries, and people but not necessarily creating a better intercultural understanding. Globalization accelerates the speed with which information, goods, and people circulate among different publics, markets, and nations, but the blurring of frontiers equally provokes national anxieties, social frictions, and cultural clashes. These propositions are also valid for Islam.

Globalization does not stop short of changing the lives and minds of Muslims; furthermore, Islam becomes an active component in the acceleration and amplification of globalism. Political Islam does not operate exclusively on a national scale but enters into a new phase of circulation at a planetary scale. In an earlier phase, the politicization of Islam, that led to the Iranian Revolution of 1979, was studied on a national scale as a mode of popular mobilization inspired by an ideology and a religious lexicon that condemn the authoritarian and "impious" powers of the Middle East. Islamic radicalism was explained as an outcome of several factors, such as immigration, economic poverty, and political regimes, as a reaction to a situation of crisis. The vertical relations of power between state and society were privileged in this earlier phase of Islamic studies. However, the scale of analysis shifted to a more transnational and global one following the terrorist attacks of 9–11 in 2001 that marked a turning point in the analysis of "global Islam."[7] Mainly the terrorist dimensions of Islamic movements are explained in conformity with the forces of globalism. The jihadism of Al-Qaeda is taken to be the most dramatic illustration of globalized Islam; its nebulous mode of organization, the profile of its terrorist-martyrs, the transnational life trajectories in their military training, as well as the targets of attack, can all be seen as the product of a transnational logic. The global imprint is quite obvious in the logic of terrorist acts or in the life trajectories of the terrorists. However, the jihadist attacks did not only follow and profit from global dynamics, but also in an unexpected and unwilling way brought the United States to join the global world and suffer its destructive effects.[8]

The centrality of the notion of *umma*, the community of believers in the Islamic faith, predisposes Muslims to think and act beyond national borders, that is, globally. Although it is quite unrealistic to evoke a unified Muslim community at a moment in history when confessional differences and national interests continue to divide Muslims,[9] contemporary Islamism does participate in the production of a common imaginary. It elaborates itself by mutual borrowings and hybridizations: the traditions and norms of a confession (such as the martyr figure in the Shiite tradition) are continuously readapted and transformed by those of other confessions, hence producing a religious and political syncretism.[10] One might argue that the production of an Islamic social imaginary takes place through micropractices, performative and visual acts that circulate between different publics and take root in different national contexts.[11] It is possible to sort out a mapping of an Islamic imaginary following a series of constitutive events that provide a common reference, repertoire of action, and collective memory. The formation of an Islamic imaginary transgresses national boundaries and preestablished confessional distinctions; it works as a collage, an assemblage bringing together distinct elements, composing with different fragments, and producing a new pattern of action. Globalization accelerates the elaboration of a social religious imaginary and its promises, providing a virtual sense of belonging, a social bondage even between those who do not share the same communitarian, confessional, or national distinctions. The sorority among veiled women or the fraternity among martyrs—even though they represent two very distinct and opposing forms of religious agency and religious figures as pious-self or self-sacrifice—embody the micropractices constitutive of this imaginary.

As Charles Taylor argues, the social imaginary is elaborated by means of religious performances, symbols, and narratives; it is mediated by a visual and popular culture.[12] Islamic social imaginary is shaped by religious piety, memory, and a repertoire of action that is both religiously and politically oriented among actors who are connected to each other by religious and imaginary ties, forming an "imagined community,"[13] and not necessarily a national one. The radicalization of Islamic political movements at the end of the 1970s was closely related to a new ideological framework that was elaborated by thinkers and ideologists of Islam. These authors were widely translated and read by the generation of Muslims who have followed the ideas of politicization of Islam and embraced the criticism addressed to orthodox religious thinkers (*ulema*). But in distinction from Islamic theology and ideology, both being shaped by the knowledge of few, by a group of theologians and political activists,

Islamic social imaginary is shaped by new forms of visual and performative culture and is shared by persons and groups who do not necessarily have a sense of belonging to a political structure or to a religious institution. However, globalized forms of Islam participate in the elaboration of a religious imaginary and cultural performance that unsettles and challenges European secular imaginaries and gendered performances.

If the political and the national are no longer the decisive mediators of conflict and consensus, how can we frame the question of religious and cultural difference? The debates on globalization necessitate a rethinking of the place of the national,[14] but likewise of the public sphere.

Islam in Public

The nature of the relationship between the political and the public spheres, their mutual interdependence, undergoes a change with the impact of globalism. By means of global communication networks, the public sphere participates in a transnational realm, whereas the political sphere is constrained and confined within the boundaries of a nation-state. Globalization instigates the autonomization of the public realm vis-à-vis that of the political. Whereas publics have the tendency to become transnational, politics remain national.

The public domain hence becomes the privileged site for the manifestations of a globalized Islam in Europe.[15] The search for the public visibility of religion triggers public controversies in different national contexts and across borders. Islam participates in the formation of a transnational European public, but in confrontation with the norms and morals of European secular modernity. The emergence of a transnational public space is accompanied by deepening of the cleavages: national publics, cultural codes, and religious references are brought into spatial proximity while cultural differences are at the same time staged, accentuated, and amplified by symbols, clichés, or grotesque images. In the age of globalism, the public sphere favors circulation rather than mediation (whether political, intellectual, or artistic), the figural rather than the textual, the affective sensorial and scandalous rather than the rational and discursive. Hence symbols, images, icons, or cartoons travel faster than words, penetrate personal and collective imaginaries, and propagate by amplification of their significations and perceptions. The public sphere becomes the site for confrontational proximity and copenetrations between different Muslim and European cultural and religious codes.

In late modernity, the spectacular and the visual figural attributes of public communication are privileged. New forms of Islamic agency follow and amplify the performative, symbolic, sensorial, and affective dimensions of expressing religious difference. Islam is staged in public by means of religious rituals and symbols, by gendered modes of address, by protests and collective prayers, and by new forms of jihadism and violence that challenge and threaten the consensual values and civilizational attributes of Europe. These acts and agencies, less discursive and more performative, employ a sort of grammar of silence, a nonverbal communication, and yet have the ability to provoke and unsettle the established relations of cultural difference and power.

A new frame of thought is necessary to conceptualize the ways European publics relate to Islamic difference. It necessitates unsettling the hegemony of the European self-presentation and conceptualization of a transversal bond without excluding the role of the confrontation, violence, and discord, namely a process of "interpenetration" between the two in which definitions of sexuality and the sacred play a central role.[16]

A mapping of events, incidents, and controversies can highlight the zones of contact and confrontation, the zones that we can also designate as "frontier spaces" between Europe and Islam.[17] The fatwa against Salman Rushdie, the public debate on the Islamic veiling in France, Ayan Hirsi Ali's film *Submission* and the assassination of Theo van Gogh, the cartoon controversy in Denmark, the attacks of Al-Qaeda in the European cities, and the debates on the Turkish candidacy to the European Union are all examples of the antagonistic nature of this encounter. Each of these events, in different ways, has carried Islam into European publics and provoked a larger debate on the cultural values and frontiers of Europe in distinction with Islam, ranging from the place of religion in public life, principles of secularism, freedom of expression, and gender equality.

The relationship established between an ideal public sphere and the functioning of a pluralistic democracy, particularly in the work of Jürgen Habermas, has been revisited from an interdisciplinary perspective in view of a more pluralistic conceptualization of the public sphere. The critiques of the public sphere have demonstrated the ways the latter reassembles and includes, as well as the ways it excludes, by means of drawing boundaries and establishing criteria of access in terms of education, class, age, gender, and race. However, Islam has been disregarded in these conceptualizations of the public sphere.[18] Adding Islam to this list does not imply simply the broadening of the boundaries of the public sphere. The irruption of Islam within European publics reveals new boundaries of exclusion but also the public doxas, namely a set of shared secular imaginaries and feminist presuppositions that are constitutive of the contemporary European public mind. Islam carries religion into public life and disrupts the preestablished boundaries between privatized religion and public rationality on the one hand and gendered definitions of agency on the other. The Islamic veiling of the schoolgirls disrupts the criteria of age, education, and gender in proscribing access to public citizenship and debate. The arguments that favored the ban on religious signs in French public schools were based generally upon the denial of agency (they are minor) and individuality of Muslim girls (they are religious) in adopting the headscarf. Furthermore, fathers, brothers, militant Islam, or community pressure are designated as the oppressor behind the symbol of the veil. Secular narratives of modernity have expected religion to withdraw into the private realm and disappear as an actor of change, of history. Consequently, the definitions of citizenship rights—namely, equal access to the public sphere, freedom of expression, liberty, and agency—are all thought to be the outcome of secular formations of individualism and power. Muslims in Europe become citizens through religious difference, which acts like a process of singularization. As Louis Quéré points out, social actors "do not pre-exist their configurations on the public stage; they take shape by incorporating symbolic mediations that are, by definition, public—that is to say, symbolic mediations that transcend individuals, are shared, accessible to all and are both observable and describable."[19] In this sense, Muslim citizens' claim for religious covering disrupts the equation between secularism and political agency but also between feminism and emancipation. Religious gendered agency reveals a series of ambivalences—faith and agency, woman and public life, age and decision—that cannot be acknowledged within the secular European frames of thinking in terms of "either-or" categories (either religious or secular, either feminist or Islamist, either European or Muslim). Public Islam blurs and unsettles not only the personal-public frontiers, and religious-secular oppositions, but moreover brings forth new borrowings, mixings, recompositions between these binary oppositions.

Sexuality and Islam

In shifting the boundaries between the personal and the political, contemporary Islam ironically joins Western feminism in many ways. The realm that is considered to be closest to the personal, corporeal, intimate, and sacred is carried into public life; wearing religious symbols in public schools, construction of mosques in European cities, dietary regimes in cafeterias, Islamic holidays, rooms for prayer in work settings, are all examples that inscribe a religious imprint on the European public spaces. The European presence of Islam takes religion into the agenda of politics but more profoundly unsettles the established boundaries between the private and the public. A religious reminder of the personal, private, and public makes its way into new agencies and imaginaries. A sacred notion of the private parts of the body and space is brought into modern public life, a process that I have designated as "modern-mahrem," or "forbidden modern." The Arabic word *mahrem* signifies the interior, sacred, gendered space, forbidden to exterior and stranger masculine gaze, which is both spatial and corporeal.[20]

The veil, an instrument of modesty, must both conceal the body and reflect gender segregation in society. The interior space, like the veil, embodies an entire theology to do with maintaining the purity of women. Paradoxically, it is the space hidden from the gaze of others, the realm of feminine intimacy that defines what is forbidden and what is not. Private—a word without a synonym in Muslim culture—refers to the sphere of the sacred, the interior, as well as to intimacy, but also to a gendered space better encapsulated by the word mahrem. The Islamic veil relates to a forbidden exterior masculine gaze on women and marks the boundaries between interior and exterior that also symbolize the segregation of the sexes. Its public manifestation challenges concerns about invisibility, modesty, and self-concealment. Veiling, covering, and headscarf are used interchangeably to designate the Islamic principle of *hijab* (the necessity for women to cover their hair, their shoulders, and the shapes of their bodies to preserve their virtue and avoid being a source of *fitna*, i.e., disorder within the community). The contemporary Islamic outfit is generally a headscarf that completely covers the hair and falls upon the shoulders (quite distinct from the traditional use of a headscarf) and a sort of long gown that hides the feminine shape. Since the 1980s, the demands by female students to be allowed to attend public schools with a headscarf has become the most debated and divisive issue in Turkey's public debate between secularists and Islamists.

The veiling of women is a reminder of an alternative way of linking femininity and sexuality in public. While feminine traits are expressed and distinguished from male outlook and male appearances (veiling is supposed to set a difference from male dress codes), a woman's sexuality is contained within the values of modesty. In contrast, the secular feminist modes of self-fashioning blur gender differences by borrowing from men's clothing and appearance (unisex and short hair as emblems of feminism) and expose the liberty of sexual disposition and interaction with the other sex. The opposition and confrontation between two figures of women reveal the differences of corporeal management of femininity and sexuality in public life. The battleground involves the orientation of aesthetical values alongside ethical ones. Inventions of new modes of Islamic covering point to the changes in the domain of fashion, through which new elaborations of beauty, femininity, and sexuality are manifested.

The question of women and sexuality occupies a central place in these controversies because late modernity is shaped by gender equality and emancipatory regimes of body and sexuality. The European self-fashioning and self-presentation embody the equality of gender relations, between women and men as well as between persons of the same sex. In the eyes of the European publics, Islamic veiling as a symbol of religious submission and gender segregation becomes a reminder of a pre-feminist past. However, the contemporary veiling is carried into public life by young women who by means of education and political engagement have distanced themselves from traditional gender roles and found themselves mixing socially with men. The veiling publicly stages a form of feminine personality and sexuality that enters into confrontation with the European self-presentations of women and secular modernity. Islamic veiling is contemporary with secular feminism and yet in oppositional distinction with the preestablished norms of secular emancipation.

For the post-1968 feminists, the body was central in the struggle for emancipation of women (as the slogan "our bodies belong to us" illustrates); a body liberated from the chains of biological difference (the right to abortion and contraception), from sexual violence and harassment, and from the male desire and gaze; a body that was taking its revenge by displaying its new liberty in public. Feminism has profoundly altered not only the relationship between women and men, but also the relationship of women with their own bodies. This process is also synonymous with the entrance of women's bodies in the spiral of an accelerated secularization in which the culture of "care of the self," "pleasing one's own self," and "taking good care of one's body" shows that the body has not only turned into a place of the cult for personal liberty but also conforms with the imperatives of neoliberalism. Yesterday's rights to contraception and abortion and today's genetic engineering have displaced the realm of reproduction from the universe of natural constraints to that of personal choice, thereby shifting the cursor from nature toward culture. This process is an undeniable sign of a larger personal liberty and plurality of options of choice in life, but it also opens up significant questioning in moral and ethical terms. The return of religion in the contemporary world is not a relic of the past but an indicator of the contemporary problems and limits raised by late or ultramodernity.

Religion in general and the act of veiling in particular recall the submission of the self to divine will and valorize the feeling of humility against the will of the secular and omnipotent modern subject. It is woman's body—as the marker of values of modesty or pleasure, submission or emancipation—that comes to intersect the patriarchal power relations and the confrontation between religious and secular women. In other words, the Enlightenment project can be read as an incessant displacement of the frontiers between nature and culture, progressively displacing the realm of religion, reproduction, and nature into the domain of the cultural and thus turning religion into a matter of individual choice; women's bodies follow the imperatives of this metaproject and delineate the cursor between the religious and the mundane, the patriarchal and the personal, the natural and the cultural.

In the act of wearing the Islamic veil, one can read a critique addressed to the logic of extreme emancipation, in which the body is the locus. Without always being the master of the signification of this act, a woman who covers her hair conveys a sense of preservation of self, a resistance to the spiral of secularization—a spiral that encompasses all domains of life from procreation to aesthetics, and that offers a distressing promise of incessant changes and innovations. In counterdistinction with Western woman's body—considered as a symbol of aesthetic prestige and liberty, an object of idolatry—Muslim women reintroduce in their subjectivity a part of abstraction through obedience to the divine order, to religious rituals and constraining mundane and carnal pleasures. (The training of the *nafs*—an Arabic word that means the flesh, the spirit of concupiscence, which symbolizes the carnal impulses—so as to make it obedient to pious impulses is central for the construction of Muslim subject.)

Islamic veiling allows Muslim women to make their appearance on the public scene as much as it conceals and confines them. It accentuates the battle of social mores by means of adopting performative but silent/nonverbal communication. It is the incarnation of Islamic religious precepts, of the social grammar of interdiction between the gaze and the body, as well as of the exposition of what is at stake in clothing and effects of "stylization." Georg Simmel argues that clothing is an "appeasing response to the exaggerated subjectivism of the époque, the place of 'retreat,' of individuals taking distance and a manifestation of a sense of modesty and discretion."[21] For clothing is about the connection of particular to the general, the personal to the impersonal, and the subjective to the intersubjective. It distinguishes and creates a distance as much as it allows the individual to enter into a form that is shared by the others. It is with these modern ways of clothing that the veiling is situated in this "in-between-ness": it is both modern and Muslim.[22] Being a modern Muslim is a state of being in-between because it reveals both proximity and alterity through the clothing of emancipated religious women and thus seeks to subvert the aesthetical definition of femininity and that of subjectivity.

Islamic studies are inseparable from the studies on modernity in its multiple, alternative, and nonoccidental forms. The more the definition of modernity is separated from the Enlightenment paradigm, the more our reflection opens up on the new forms and criticisms that modernity takes on today. This fact weakens the Western narratives on modernity at work in the social sciences today. At the same time it blurs the frontiers between the social sciences of the "other" (Orientalism, area studies, anthropology, postcolonial studies) and the social sciences of the (Western) "self" (history, sociology, political science, and feminism). Islamic studies are at the heart of this metamorphosis in social sciences as both subject and instigator of this transformation. The gendered, public, and global manifestations of Muslim piety challenge the studies on Islam to open up a new space for reading Western modernity and decolonizing European sociology. Islam and Islamic studies can be thought of as a necessary antinomy, as the "constitutive outside" to the public doxas of secular-sexual modernity.[23] To the extent that they contribute to the unpacking of these Eurocentric doxas of sexual norms, public morals, and global order, Islamic studies have the potential to subvert social scientific agenda and reorient social criticism.

3 Religious-Secular Frontiers

State, Public Sphere, and the Self

Contemporary Islamic studies weaken the centrality of Western narratives on modernity at work in the social sciences. It is now necessary to make a succinct mental mapping of the changes, shifts, and displacements that are currently taking place in our ways of approaching the secular-religious divide. Here I undertake an analysis and selective reassessment of the changes that have occurred during the last three decades in our approaches to secularism. Due to our ongoing conversations across cultures and disciplines, there is an increasing awareness in the social sciences that there is not one ideal model of secularism, whether it is defined by the Anglo-Saxon liberal model or by the French political *laïcité*, but there exists a plurality of secularisms in different national, cultural, and religious contexts, including the non-Western secularisms, such as the Indian and the Turkish ones. The point of departure is the necessity of decoupling secularism and Western experience and acknowledging the plurality of secularisms. In this way, we can foster a comparative gaze between different genealogies, historical trajectories, cultural habitations, and political formations of the secular. However, in order to understand the present-day forces of the religious-secular formations and confrontations, it is not enough to emphasize only the plurality of secularisms that supposes distinct national formations and cultural crossings. We should shed equal light on the interconnected histories of secularism.

It is not therefore sufficient to open our readings of secularism to its multiple configurations in distinct national formations as if they are independent from each other. The formations of the secular follow different historical trajectories and have different religious genealogies in different places, yet they are closely interconnected with the hegemonic impositions of the Western modernity and colonialism. The revival of religious movements, conservative values, various fundamentalisms, and in particular the Islamist movements challenge the authoritarian modes of secularism that exclude religion from public life and from definitions of modern self. New modes of confrontation are taking place between the secular and the religious but also across cultures and civilizations.

Coupling the incomparable, namely the French and Turkish examples, in spite of their differences, can help us understand the intercivilizational encounters of the secular. The two different historical experiences, European and non-European, with two different religious genealogies, Christian and Muslim, following two different trajectories of nation-state building, democratic and authoritarian, are historically connected to each other by the principle of laïcité. Both countries cherish republican secularism, and idealize a public life exempt from religious signs, yet both witnessed in the last thirty years the rise of Islamic visibility in public life and a destabilization of the established boundaries between the secular and the religious, leading to a process of confrontation, rivalry, and mimicry between the two. If the Turkish secularism, *laiklik*, is derived from the French laïcité and from dialogical encounters with Western civilization, today the debates on French secularism are engaged in relation to Islamic presence in Europe. The Islamic headscarf issue crystallizes, both in France and in Turkey, the debates on the presence of religious visibility in the public life, the civilizational aspect of the confrontation, and the enforcement of republican secularism by law-making or by the support of the army.

The first point that needs to be emphasized is that the Western master narrative of secularism undergoes a radical change as it shifts from an "indigenous" debate that is shaped by exchanges with Christian religion to that of confrontation with Islam. The second shift concerns the acknowledgment of the plurality of secularisms and to a growing interest in depicting and understanding non-Western forms of secularity. As discussed in chapter 2, the master narrative of Western secularity has imposed a sociological gaze that has evaluated the non-European experiences with an established set of criteria and has measured the inconsistencies or deficiencies in respect to a model that is supposed to be universal. However, the studies of the secular have introduced the idea that secularity is a *longue durée* history of reforms that initially had their loci within the religion itself and hence deconstructed the religious-free approaches to secularism. Marcel Gauchet's work that elucidates the particular role Christianity played in the process of secularity (Christianity as "the religion of the end of religion") is a pioneer in rearticulating the secular with the religious.[1] In his recent work, Charles Taylor addresses a critique to the narrative of secularism that dismisses the changes that have occurred in the religious and spiritual realm and argues against what he calls "subtraction theories" that define secularity as minus religion and hence tells the story of a secular age as it develops within and out of Latin Christianity.[2]

Such approaches shift the interest to the religious context in which secularism evolves and thereby lead to an unpacking of secularity as a religious-free, neutral, and universal development of European modernity. Revealing the particularity of secularism and its intrinsic relation to Christianity goes hand in hand with a critique of universalist claims of a Western model of secular modernity. These criticisms have an impact on the ways we de-center the European view of secularism and open our readings to the multiplicity of secularisms. Consequently we can adopt two different attitudes in studying secularism in non-Western contexts. Either we postulate that secularism is the product of Western history, intrinsic to Latin Christendom and consequently an alien ideology for the non-Western civilizations (as Bernard Lewis argues for Islamic civilization).[3] Or, on the contrary, we decouple the secular and the Western and study the multiple formations and manifestations of the secular in different historical and religious contexts.

However, both positions are problematic because they ignore the impact of Western secular modernity, the way it travels to different contexts, by different political forms of interaction, such as colonialism or modernism, the Indian and Turkish secularism being typical examples. They illustrate the manifold manifestations of secularism in relation to two different nation-building processes—the former shaped by the postcolonial and the latter by the post-Empire context—and in relation to Hindu and Muslim religious genealogies. The multiple forms of secularism, namely the Hindu and Turkish secularisms, are shaped on the one hand by the formations of the national and on the other by the dialogical relations with the religious and the modern. In our readings of multiple secularisms in non-Western contexts, we cannot ignore the way secularity is transmitted as a vector of the Western way of life, as a way of self and public governance. Although one cannot dismiss the imprint of colonialism and modernism in shaping the formations of the secular, one cannot reduce the latter to a mere copy of Western secularism.

In order to depict and translate the particularity of Muslim (or Hindu) habitations of the secular, we need to give up "deficiency theory," presupposing that the non-Western experiences are lagging behind, incomplete, and noncontemporaneous of the West. Secularism in non-Western contexts is often conceptualized as a second-rank imitation of the Western original. That is how Turkish secularism is often studied as an authoritarian derivative of French laïcité, measured in terms of its gaps, inconsistencies, and deficiencies with regard to the French ideal model. Whereas each time a notion travels, and is repeated, it is never exactly the same because in the process of repeating a term or a concept, we never simply produce a replica of the original usage; every reiteration transforms the original, adding new meanings to it.[4] The French notion of laïcité is readopted to Turkish language as laiklik and thereby becomes part of daily political usage and collective imaginary. The use of the same notion with a slight change of the accent points to a process of iteration in which the workings of the secular power go beyond being a mere second-rank copy and add new meanings, discourses, images, and practices. Instead of reading secularity in the mirror of an ideal Western model and measuring its gaps and deficiencies, we need to depict the ways secularism is semantically adopted, politically reinvented, collectively imagined, and legally institutionalized.

We are witnessing the weakening of the hegemony of the secular not only as a master narrative in social sciences and as an ideology of the Western modernity but also as a collective imaginary that regulates daily social lives of individuals. The decline of the power of the secular signifies that the old hierarchical boundaries with the religious are unsettled and become more porous. Rather than capturing the relation between the two in consecutive terms, as religion alternating with the secular, and pointing to a postsecular era, we need to understand the ways religion becomes contemporaneous with the secular modern.[5] We can hitherto speak of the recompositions of the religious-secular divide as well as new confrontations, rivalry, and mimicry between the two. The religious-secular divide manifests and competes, as I argue, at three levels, namely the state, public sphere, and self. The battleground between the religious and the secular concerns foremost the formation of the state, the governance of the public sphere, and the ethics of self.

Monopoly of the State over the Religious-Secular Distinctions

We speak of distinct models of secularism as nation-wide, such as French, American, Indian, and Turkish secularisms. The story of secularism can hardly be told independent of the history of nation-state building. Secularism understood as a principle of separation between state and religion underpins the nation-state building process, based on man-made laws as opposed to God-centered, sacred ones, and popular sovereignty. There are two widespread tacit beliefs that are increasingly questioned. First, secularism and democracy are thought to be concomitant with each other. Second, secularism is understood as the impartiality of the state and therefore as guarantee of religious and confessional pluralism and atheism. Both presuppositions run counter to particular historical experiences. Secularism can foster liberal pluralism or authoritarian nationalism; it depends on the trajectories of a given nation-building process.

In the Turkish case, although the debates and the process of secularization concerning norms, laws, and institutions started during the second half of the nineteenth century in the Ottoman Empire, secularism reached its apogee with the Turkish state-building process after 1923 and became the founding ideology of republican nationalism.[6] It created its own national elites by means of a compulsory nationwide secular education and the adoption of Latin script. Hence Turkish secularism works within the frame of politics of uniformization and homogenization of a national culture against the legacy of a multiethnic and multireligious Ottoman Empire.[7] The eradication of non-Muslim minorities, by population exchanges and massacres in the last days of the empire and during the first decades of the republic, led to a social terrain in which Sunnite Islam became the religion of majority. Secularism underpinned the ideal of a national community "free of religion," yet implicitly defined as a Muslim and Sunnite majority, distinct from non-Muslim minorities of the cosmopolitan empire as well as the Alevis and Kurds.

In the process of Turkish nation-state building, secularism became a vector for the homogenization of a national culture, whereas in the case of India, secularism is enacted as a guarantee of religious pluralism. In both cases, secularism plays an important role as a state ideology, and the state is declared a secular state in both Indian and Turkish Constitutions. However, the context of state-building becomes decisive in the meanings and practices of secularism. In India, anticolonial resistance privileged cultural and religious differences, whereas in Turkey the dismantling of a multireligious and multiethnic empire led to the making of a national community. Secularism as a guarantee for religious pluralism in India and for modern nationalism in Turkey played different roles. If today Hindu nationalism challenges national diversity and the legacy of religious pluralism in India, in Turkey political Islam challenges authoritarian and exclusionary politics of secular nationalism.

Islamic movements cultivate an ambivalent relation with nationalism. Islamic critical thought and political radicalism were first developed against the supremacy of the national, defending the community of believers (umma) as a main reference for collective identity of Muslims. However, Islam becomes also a form of nationalism.[8] Islamic revolution in Iran in 1979 can be interpreted as a way of completing the nation-state building process, ending the monarchy, centralizing religious education, and homogenizing the national culture by religion, but also providing a forceful symbolic and political example of Islam as an organized state power. In many respects, one should compare Turkish and Iranian examples as reverse mirroring. Turkish republican secularism and the figure of Atatürk have been taken as an exemplary model and a source of inspiration in many Muslim countries, including in Iran. Hence social science literature compares Turkey and Iran in their respective engagements with secularization synonymous of Westernization. However, the comparison between the two countries can also be made in relation to their formations of the national. Turkey ended Ottoman monarchy and realized the transition to a nation-state within the ideological framework of secularism in 1923, whereas Iran ended the power of the monarchy with an Islamic revolution in 1979. Both countries are republican states; but the secular-religious divide is reversed, the former completed the formation of the national by means of political secularism (laiklik), the latter by means of political Islamism. The organized state power is framed by national secularism in Turkey and by national Islamism in Iran. In both countries pluralism and democracy signify the distancing and autonomy of the state in regard to the political ideology of secularism and Islamism. What is at stake is the decline of the hegemony of the state over the definitions of the secular and the religious. The changes cannot be captured in terms of linear, consecutive, and alternating replacements between the secular and the religious. Rather than either-or arguments, Islamization versus democratization, one has to frame the changes in terms of recompositions and mutual borrowings between the secular and the religious. The process of democratization in Turkey shows that despite the political polarization between the religious and the secular, the wall of separation between the two becomes more and more porous; mutual borrowings and cross-fertilizations blur the rigid distinctions. Hence it is difficult to speak of clear-cut distinctions between the projects of the secular and the Islamic. The Islam-rooted AKP (Party of Justice and Development) government took on the project of European Union and enhanced a series of reforms for the recognition of ethnic and religious pluralism, while the political parties of secular-legacy turned toward nationalism and anti-European politics. It would be too simplistic to interpret the Islamic politics in Turkey as the failure of secularism, as it likewise would be to interpret the opposition movements in Iran as the end of Islam. The democratic resistance and protest movements in Iran during the general elections in May 2009 criticized the theocratic power as abandoning the original ideals of the revolution and called for the end of the monopoly of the state over the definitions of Islam.[9] In spite of different levels of pluralism and democracy, in both cases we witness that the political distinctions of the religious-secular divide are unsettled. And in both cases nationalism plays an inhibiting role in claiming the monopoly of the state over the definitions of either the secular or the religious.

The reconfigurations between the secular and the religious are shaped not only by nation-states but also by transnational dynamics and global migratory flows. European nation-states have become gradually migrant, multireligious, and culturally heterogeneous. The established division between pious America and secular Europe does not hold any longer. Muslim migrants in Europe or Polish citizens of Europe claim freedom of religion. The European Union remembers its spiritual roots and Christian heritage to define its Constitution, cultural unity, and geographic frontiers. Is Europe secular or Christian? What about Muslims and Jews living in Christian Europe? Whether three monotheistic religions define equally the European heritage, or is Judeo-Christian Europe distinguished from the Islamic other? Do the debates over the legitimacy of Turkish membership in the European Union reveal a religious difference or a civilizational one? Turkish membership bringing forth both Muslim and secular affiliations unsettles the established boundaries of European identity, whether they are defined in cultural or religious terms.

On the other hand, Muslim migrants claim their Islamic visibility in the European public sphere while they distance themselves from the national origins of their religion. The way Islamic religion is learned, interpreted, and practiced in Europe is a novel experience to the extent that it is not in direct continuity with the "parents' religion" nor affiliated with a given nation. Islam becomes part of disembedded, imagined forms of horizontal solidarity. Charles Taylor describes social disembeddedness as a condition for a different kind of social imaginary; that is, "horizontal forms of social imaginary in which people grasp themselves and great numbers of others as existing and acting simultaneously."[10] To the extent that European Islam is disembedded from national cultures, it becomes a religious experience both in individual and collective terms, leading to new hybrid forms between secular Europe and religious Muslims. Once again we witness the unsettlement of the distinctions between Islam and Europe, between religious and secular. New recompositions, tensions, copenetrations between the two give rise to new definitions of self and everyday life practices.

The story of secularism is not confined to a given nation-state but follows a transnational dynamic in which the encounters and confrontations among different cultures and civilizations become paramount in shaping debates, unsettling distinctions, and accelerating borrowings between the secular and the religious.

Secular and Pious Self

Secularism is a mode of state governance as well as a set of moral values for the governance of the self. Secularism works as an organizing principle of social life, penetrates into everyday life practices, and underpins the politics of emancipation and sexuality. In non-Western contexts, secularism is closely interrelated with the "civilizing mission" of the West and transmits a set of norms that define rationality as well as ethical and aesthetical forms. Colonial or modernist elites embody such norms by means of their access to Western ways of rational thinking and life practices. The norms of Western civilization are transmitted and adopted at the level of everyday life practices, definitions of self and habitus. The creation of a secular habitus in a Muslim majority country means a series of changes in traditional and religious culture that brings women to the forefront as markers of new life. Practices and reforms such as abandoning the veil, compulsory coeducation, social mixing of men and women, free love, equal rights for men and women, women's performance in public, all denote the changes against the traditional-religious norms of women's covering, the ban on women's performance and visibility on the public scene, gender segregation in social life, arranged marriages, and polygamy.

Secular self means a set of bodily practices to be learned, rehearsed, and performed, ranging from ways of dressing (and undressing), talking, and socializing with men, to behaving in public. The habitations of the secular are not transmitted naturally and implicitly, but on the contrary become part of a project of modernity and politics of the self that require assimilation and acculturation to a Western culture.

The changes in dress codes are particularly charged with political symbolism. Two figures who were the incarnation of Turkish and Indian independence, both known as the "father" of the nation, namely Kemal Atatürk and Mahatma Gandhi, communicated in their public lives and ways of clothing their commitments to the local and Western cultures, traditional and modern, spiritual and secular distinctions. Both men in different ways embodied the governance of the self and governance of the public. Both leaders performed their clothing preferences publicly and symbolically. Atatürk opted for Western-style clothes (his wardrobe is still exhibited in his mausoleum in Ankara), whereas Gandhi wore the traditional Indian *dhoti* (fabric made from local traditional raw cotton) and shawl.[11] Gandhi ate simple vegetarian food and practiced fasting as a means of self-purification. Atatürk avoided any spiritual activity in public, instigating a role model to be followed by Turkish secular politicians, who abstained from the use of any religious idiom and practice, including fasting during the month of Ramadan. One represented "religious disobedience" and expressed the desire to belong to the home of civilized (read Western) nations; the other manifested "civil disobedience" and resistance to colonial powers of the West. While Gandhi ended untouchability in India, Atatürk advocated women's participation in public life and replaced Sharia law with Swiss Civil Code to ensure gender equality. The abolition of the Caliphate (the Ottoman Emperor as Caliph was the supreme religious and political leader of all Sunni Muslims across the world) in 1924 by the pro-Western nationalist movement of Atatürk connected the histories of the two countries in an unprecedented way. The dismemberment of the Ottoman Empire and the end of the Caliphate system evoked sympathy among Indian Muslims but also among the members of the Indian independence movement, leading to political and social mobilization on behalf of the Ottoman Caliphate, known as the "Khilafat movement" in India.

One can establish a relationship between the end of the Caliphate and the renewal of Islamic movements. The abolition of the Caliphate engenders a vacuum of religious authority and disunity in the Muslim world, and since the end of the 1970s has led to a plethora of Islamic movements competing with each other over the interpretations of religious norms and political authority.[12] The revolution in Iran and the establishment of Islam as an organized state power provides a model of political reference and aspiration for contemporary Islamist movements, but the state-oriented political agenda of these movements should not overshadow the cultural-religious repertoire. Contemporary actors of Islam are engaged critically with the cultural program of secular modernity and Western colonialism.

Islamic movements challenge the established equation between definitions of Western self and civilized self, elaborating an alternative performative politics of pious self and habitus in modern contexts.[13] Religion becomes part of interpretation and improvisation for self-definitions of Muslims who seek to restore piety in modern life. Individuation (more precisely personalization) of religion goes hand in hand with the establishment of collective bonds among Muslims who recognize each other by means of a shared repertoire of performative piety.

In the revival of religious movements, there is an element of Islamic "self-fashioning" that follows the dynamics of modern individuation.[14] As Stephen Greenblatt argues, the modern individuation is not boundless, and the fashioning of the self is the outcome of the mechanisms of discipline, restraint, and a partial suppression of the personality. Similarly, Islam provides an alternative repertoire for self-fashioning and self-restraint by means of disciplinary practices, which range from supervision of the imperatives of faith and control of sexuality, both in mind and body, called *nafs* in Islam. The Islamic headscarf expresses the self-fashioning of Muslim girls with disciplinary categories of Islam but for whom the category of faith is not prearranged and enters into the domain of improvisation, adaptation, and invention. It is a sign of self-restraint (*hijab* means modest behavior and dress) and self-fashioning, including in literal terms the production of Islamic aesthetics and fashion.

Islamic self-fashioning and self-governance confronts contemporary secular feminism. A nonverbal but embodied communication in the veil conveys a sense of disobedience to secular notions of self-formation and sexual freedom. If the Islamic veil, by covering a woman's body, is a reminder of sacred intimacy in public, secular feminism claims equality and transparency in bringing the personal and the intimate into public. If covered women remind us of the limits of sexuality and nonavailability of Muslim women in public, the uncovered women interpret emancipation as the free display of desire and body in public. When it is not enforced on women by state power or communitarian pressure, and when it expresses the personal trajectories of women and their self-fashioning piety, the Islamic veil presents a critique of secular interpretation of women's emancipation. Islamic feminism unsettles the religious-secular divide to the extent that Muslim women are both pious and public, blurring the distinctions between religion and gender effacement. There is a reverse mirroring between pious and secular self-fashioning, but in each case the boundaries between personal and public, self and sexuality, religious and secular become fuzzy as they are intertwined with each other.

Secular Public Spaces and Religious Visibilities

The claims of religious visibility in public and the controversies they provoke reveal the unspoken secular rules and norms of the public sphere in European countries. There are different levels of state control over the religious presence in public life, ranging from active and aggressive to more pluralistic conceptions of secularism, depending on the national politics.[15] The question of religion in the public sphere, however, cannot be reduced to choices of liberal versus authoritarian politics of secularism. French and Turkish policies that banned the Islamic headscarf in the public schools (France) and in the universities (Turkey)[16] can be considered as exclusionary and active, if not an authoritarian interpretation of laïcité. However, the two countries are not exceptional in debating and attempting to restrain Islamic presence in the public sphere. In Germany and Italy, where the public presence of religion is not as unwanted as in France, the polarizing debates on the construction of mosques, the height of the minarets, and the shape of the domes, reveal the disturbing irruption of Islamic visibility in the public landscape.[17] The question of religious difference cannot be solely framed in terms of abstract principles of toleration and recognition of the plurality of faith. The question of religious difference appears in a materialized form and in a given physical space. The incursion of religious signs, symbols, and behavior (headscarf, minarets, gender segregation) disturbs the European public eye and collective consciousness to the extent that these are considered not to be in conformity with unspoken secular norms of public life. The spaces in which Muslims make their religious difference visible, such as public schools, urban places, and swimming pools, are subject to public controversy and recomposition.

With migratory dynamics and global technologies of communication, the public sphere escapes the grip of nation-states and becomes a site for transnational flows of communication, bringing in close interaction different cultures and civilizations. The public sphere that was conceptualized in relation to the European historical development of nation-states as a mononational and monolinguistic entity becomes a site of migration, religious pluralism, and civilizational encounter. How can we rethink the public sphere without reducing the public to a mononational community or to its confinement with state legislation?

The weakening of the hegemony of the national-secular calls for a new conceptualization of commonness without the vertical hierarchy of the nation-state as a prerequisite of the public sphere. The notion of space needs to be at the forefront of our analysis to depict the recompositions between secular and religious. The notion of space does not refer to an empty space but to a space of production of social relations, defining boundaries of exclusion and inclusion, of the acceptable and forbidden. A space is always regulated by certain norms, whether religious or secular. These norms are not only dictated by state law but are also shared values by those who inhabit and utilize those places. The unspoken norms are revealed once they are challenged by the intrusion of newcomers, foreigners, by those who are not supposed to be present in those spaces. The Islamic intrusion, by not being in conformity with European norms of publicness, provokes controversy and confrontation by means of which the secular and civilizational norms of public life are disclosed. However, confrontations create a new public; they bring together, in unintended and unpredictable ways, dissonant, competing persons, cultures, foreigners in proximity, in assembly. They create a new space, an interstice that affects the meanings of the religious and secular modern. The wall of separation between the two becomes porous and religious-secular distinctions become fuzzy in the course of common and confrontational public experience.

At the level of everyday life practices, individuals not only appropriate new ways of combining secular and religious norms but also choose among spiritual experiences, convert to other religions, or take from different religiosities, producing new forms of syncretism. Buddhist Catholics and also Yogi Muslims are among such nascent examples. The spatial proximity among cultures and religions creates anxiety, confusion of boundaries, and sporadic violence. But it also opens up possibilities for new ways of connecting between cultures and religions once the hegemony over definitions of religious and secular distinctions, civilized and uncivilized taxonomies, declines.

Nationalism, public sphere, and definitions of self are mainly conceptualized within the secular paradigm. I argue that the revival of religion is concomitant with the loss of hegemony of the secular at these three levels of social organization: state, public sphere, and the governance of the self. Consequently the secular-religious divide is unsettled, leading to mirroring and rivalry between the two for the orientation of the norms of the disciplinary practices of self, state, and public life. Rather than sequential replacement of one with another, of the secular with the religious, and the assertion of some kind of categorical identity, we need to think in terms of confrontations as well as recompositions between the two. Only such a paradigmatic shift can open the possibility of addressing normative questions of modernity from an intercultural perspective in which the notions of secular and religious distinctions are not derived exclusively from the Western experience.

4 Web of Secular Power

Civilization, Space, and Sexuality

The renewal of interest in secularism owes much empirically to the introduction of Islam into the picture. The religious revival of Islam and its visibility in secular spaces of modernity brought to attention various definitions of the secular. The notions of *secular, secularism, laïcité,* and *secularization* refer to different meanings and historical processes. Secularization and modernization were thought to be inseparable universal formations—an equation that today is open to increasing criticism.[1] Secularization refers to a long-term societal process through which the domain of religion is withdrawn from the realm of everyday life, changing practices of art, sexuality, and rationality. Secularity is linked to Taylor's notion of the "immanent frame," a notion that provides an unformulated background to our thinking that makes us believe that the secular order is given, and therefore it appears to us as natural. Talal Asad illustrates the connections between the secular as an epistemic category and secularism as a political doctrine.[2] French laïcité and Turkish laiklik are mainly approached as particular forms of political secularism that are assertive and exclusionary practices of the religious.

In *A Secular Age*, Taylor undertakes the task of reflecting on a longue durée history of secularity in Latin Christendom. His work proposes an alternative to the understanding of secularity as an outcome of modernity, locating its origins in the religious transformations that occurred throughout the history of Western Christianity. Against the dominant thesis of dualistic and simplistic oppositions between religion and secularity that are framed in consecutive and alternating historical phases, such as secularization, the triumph of religion, and postsecularism, Taylor engages a complex reading of the interconnections between and recompositions of the religious-secular divide, which end up, according to him, in mutual "fragilization" in the present stage. He opens up new ways of reading the religious and the antireligious as contemporary with each other, and hence distances himself from a linear sociological thesis of secularity and modernity. The uncoupling of the two permits him to speak of Western secularity in its own terms without making a claim for a universal ideal model. He acknowledges the "multiple modernities" and different patterns of secularism in other parts of the world, but he makes it explicit from the very beginning that his scope is limited and he is interested in what is unique in the experience of the West. It is inappropriate to regard his approach as ethnocentric; however, as I argue here, an introspective reading of Western secularity can lose sight of the cultural powers of the secular. The notion of the West becomes too limited if the internal history of secularity in Latin Christendom is thought to be unrelated to the processes by which colonialism developed.[3] It is therefore a matter of recognizing not the plurality of historical trajectories and patterns of secularity but the enlargement of the notion of the West and a cross-cultural and cross-civilizational approach. Western secularity cannot be separated from its claim for a higher form of civilization, its impact in shaping and stigmatizing a certain understanding of religion (as backward), its role in spreading models of secular governance to different parts of the world, and, last but not least, its permeation of material culture in norms of sexuality and private-public distinctions. I will try to illuminate such blind spots in an inwardly West-looking narrative of the secular, which can be regarded as the civilizational, sexual, and spatial powers of the secular.

The civilizing missions of the secular are manifested in the shaping of non-Western historical processes by means of colonialism and Orientalism. We cannot therefore complete the picture of secularity unless we posit it in terms of interdependence between the West and its Oriental other or colonized counterpart. Critiques of European inwardness do not simply suggest a genealogy of secularity in different historical contexts or stress a plurality of secularisms. Limiting the narration of secularity to Latin Christendom dismisses the civilizational powers of Western modernity, which are inseparable from sexual and spatial politics. Although Taylor acknowledges the importance and correspondence of the disciplinary revolution and secularity, he does not link it with the civilizational claim of the West, namely its claim of superiority in mundane life, norms of sexuality, and cultural habitus.

Furthermore, the location of secularity in a series of developments in Latin Christendom and hence the comprehension of secularity as a perspective that grew within religion—

specifically within Christianity—remain a genealogical reading, without offering a key for uncoupling Christianity and secularity. Consequently, in privileging the long-term connections between secularity and Christianity, current transformations of European secularity as it encounters other religions, in particular Islam, are kept oddly outside the picture.

Bringing Islam into our readings of European secularity is not an unproblematic move; it requires a criticism of the universalistic underpinnings of the secular and its equation with the European experience. In fact, secularism as a universal, value-free, culturally disembodied phenomenon is scrutinized and criticized by many in the social sciences. The particular link between secularism and Christianity is explored by philosophical and historical approaches other than Taylor's, which offer a critique of universalist claims of the secular. Marcel Gauchet, for instance, depicted the ways secularism is transformed from within Christianity. His approach to secularism, critical of universalist claims, opened up a realm of plurality in the societal sphere.[4] The neutrality claims of secularism have also been criticized by Etienne Balibar, who illustrated the Catholic underpinnings of secularism, which he named "catho-laïcité."[5] Talal Asad's work on the formations of the secular offers a radical twist on and criticism of the universal claims of the secular underlying the power of the European states in their relations with Muslim immigration.[6] Non-Western forms of secularism, including different models of secular authoritarianism or pluralism, such as Turkish and Indian as I discussed earlier, are also subject to new comparative research and attention, bringing to the academic agenda the multiple workings of the secular in non-Western contexts.

How does a Muslim experience of secularity transform and question our understanding of the secular age? How can one go beyond the limits of the local, particular qualifications and religious boundaries and address critiques of the "common" knowledge of secularism? The gist of the matter is, who has access to the "universal"—what kind of agencies are considered to be bound by a particular culture and locality and what kinds of others are considered to bear a universal significance? In other words, the taxonomies between the universal and the particular are not power-free, autonomous domains of knowledge.[7] Critiques of secularity therefore necessitate bringing into the picture those voices, practices, and experiences that are classified as particularistic, religious, traditional, that are not in conformity with the universal norms of secular modernity. My suggestion for reading the secular in relation to Islam is drawn not from totally outside but, on the contrary, from close encounters, confrontations, and copenetrations of Islam and secularity. I focus on the interdependence of the two, rather than setting apart a particular tradition that is supposed to be authentically different from or immune to the "secular age," and propose a reading of secularity by means of a displacement of the perspective toward Islam.

Religious claims of Muslims living in Europe invigorated the debates on secularism. As a result, European secularity and the religion of Islam can no longer be considered separate from and indifferent to each other; the two are becoming closely interrelated and mutually transformed in the present day. Some aspects of (Western) secularism come to our attention only if we bring into the picture European Muslim perspectives. In other words, the contemporary powers of the secular are not working in monocivilizational terms; they have become a matter of intercivilizational conversation.

The headscarf debate illustrates the ways in which secularity is debated in intercivilizational terms. This debate has occupied a central place mainly in two countries, Turkey and France, two secular republics that have radically different historical trajectories and patterns of secularism.[8] The Turkish heritage of political authoritarianism and the role of the army in secular politics bear a different weight from the legacy of individual freedom and liberties that has shaped the history of France. The place of Islam is not symmetrical at all in the two cases: Turkey is a Muslim-majority country, whereas France is a Muslim-migrant one. Historical (repressed) memories are also very different: the transition from the multiethnic and multireligious Ottoman Empire to a Turkish Sunni majority in the building of a nation-state created a heavy legacy of the loss of cosmopolitanism and acts of ethnic cleansing; in France, it is the unacknowledged legacy of the colonial past that underpins the present relations of French society with its Muslim migrants. French and Turkish patterns of laïcité are compared and contrasted mainly as state secularisms. The varying degrees of tolerance for religious plurality and the two nations' respective tendencies for exclusionary, assertive, if not authoritarian politics of laïcité are treated comparatively in the recent literature.[9]

Turkish secularism is often depicted as an authoritarian derivative of French laïcité, measured in terms of its gaps, inconsistencies, and deficiencies with regard to the ideal model of French secularism. However, the Turkish adaptation of laïcité involves a process of repetition in which the workings of the secular power go beyond imitations and add new meanings, discourses, images, and practices. The linguistic twist, namely laiklik, widely in use in public and political discourse in Turkey illustrates well the vernacular habitations of the secular. By coupling the incomparable—Turkish and French secularism—one is invited to engage in an interdependent mirror reading of the two instead of measuring the gap between them or the deficiencies of the former in the ideal image called "French exceptionalism." Following the questions raised by Taylor, one can go beyond the political level of comparing state secularisms and understand the ways that (voluntary) secularism takes place at the level of presentation of the ("civilized") self and the phenomenology of everyday modern life. The headscarf debate draws into our view the importance of space, material culture, bodily habitus, gender, and sexuality—the implicit powers of European secularity.

The Refashioning of Secularity: The Headscarf Debate

The first debate on the Islamic headscarf took place in 1989, in Creil, a Parisian suburb, when three young female students came to school wearing headscarves and were refused entry by the school authorities.[10] During the first debate, a regulation was issued by the minister of education, François Bayrou (called the circulaire Bayrou), that banned students from wearing ostentatious religious signs in public schools. The word *ostentatious* reappeared ten years later, in the fall 2003 debate. But the decision of whether to exclude the girls was then left to the interpretation of the school authorities. The public debate on the same issue that took place in fall 2003, in a much more passionate, widely shared, and long-lasting way, ended in the passage of legislation on March 15, 2004, that banned the Islamic headscarf, along with other religious signs, from the public schools. A semantic shift occurred between the two debates, from "headscarf affair" to "Islamic veiling," indicating a move toward a more religious designation and presentation of Muslims in France.

During the second headscarf debate that occupied the forefront of the French public scene in 2003 and 2004, one often heard the phrase "Secularism cannot be reduced to a piece of cloth" [On ne peut réduire la laïcité à un bout de tissu]. This expression conveyed the resentment and apprehension of those who were witnessing a debate that had started with the religious claims of some female Muslim migrant students to cover their heads while attending public schools. Progressively it was transformed into a more general debate on the meanings of French laïcité. An issue that was thought to be confined to regulations in the public schools later included hospitals and prisons and ended up as a debate on the secular values and foundations of the public sphere in general.

For many, secularism cannot be reduced to the headscarf issue because the claims over the headscarf appear to be a minor, trivial issue compared with the long-term historical heritage, philosophical definitions, and juridical underpinnings of French laïcité as a shared social value. Many feared that opening secularism to public debate would mean giving up cultural singularity, referred to as "French exceptionalism." Secularism is understood as a principle of the French Republic that guarantees the neutrality of the public sphere, in which citizens are expected to bracket their ethnic, religious, or class origins. The public school represents the pillar of secular republicanism, a place where, ideally speaking, "particularistic" identities, whether they stem from regional, cultural, religious, or ethnic differences, are to be replaced by a common language, memory, and education. Both instructors and students are expected to be distanced from their traditional, particularistic differences in entering the classroom and to embrace French secular values of citizenship, prerequisites for freedom, critical thinking, and dialogue. The way Islam appeared in the public schools— namely, gendered and covered, making religious-ethnic difference visible—disrupted the republican picture of French secularism. It meant the failure of the French Republic to integrate its migrants and accommodate Muslim difference. Finally, the phrase "Secularism cannot be reduced to a piece of cloth" conveyed the commitment and determination of the French not to yield secularism to new religious claims, especially not to girls who, by adopting the headscarf, contest not only the secular neutrality of the public schools but also the French notion of gender equality.

For more than two years the headscarf debate occupied a central place in the public arena and fueled the collective passions of French society in defense of secularism. Commissions were created, with politicians, feminists, experts on Islam, historians, legislators, and spokespersons of migrant communities, to investigate the state of secularism in France. The Stasi Commission, named after its chairman, Bernard Stasi, then the minister of education, was to examine the application of the principle of secularism in the republic. The status of the commission and the role it played in the public debate require particular attention. It indicated the presence of the state and its way of intervention by nominating a sort of "enlightened public," the members of which are called "the wise people" [les sages]. Among the members were public servants, experts on Islam, historians, sociologists, businessmen, representatives of nongovernmental associations, and interfaith personalities. After five months of intensive work and a series of semiprivate hearings, the commission published a report, "Laïcité et République" (December 11, 2003), and presented its recommendations, which had been adopted almost unanimously (only one member, the historian and specialist in French secularism Jean Bobérot, dissented). The commission served by and large to legitimate the law to ban the headscarf for the enforcement of secularism. In fact, the report acknowledged changes in the sociological makeup of France caused by migration and by the presence of Muslims and advised an opening up (to a certain extent) of the interpretation of secularism to a multicultural reality. It proposed, for instance, that the calendar be changed to include a major vacation for each monotheistic religion in France. However, such propositions were dismissed both by the public at large and by the lawmakers.[11]

The public, the media, and the government all converged in the view that French secularism was endangered and that a new law was required (enacted on March 15, 2004) to prohibit any sign or clothing that indicated a student's religious affiliation in public schools. The law banned all religious signs that were to be considered conspicuous, such as Christian crosses and Jewish yarmulkes as well as the Islamic headscarf. Although the law mentioned all "conspicuous signs" without singling out the headscarf, everyone agreed that it was mainly designed to discourage Muslim girls from wearing headscarves. The ban has been enforced in the public schools without major opposition from Muslim girls. This leads many to think that the headscarf is no longer an issue in French society and the new legislation helped to resolve it. I think we need to pursue a closer investigation of the consequences of the law on the educational choices of Muslim girls and whether it leads to silence or helps to express their perceptions of self, religion, and French citizenship.

John Bowen's book *Why the French Don't Like Headscarves* attempts to answer this puzzling question and meticulously details the various debates that led to the lawmaking process and the ban. He argues that secularism is not a fixed, well-defined legal and cultural framework but a narrative framework that permits public figures—politicians, journalists, and public intellectuals—to debate what laïcité should be and how Muslims living in France ought to act. His work helps us understand the power of the secular discourses and the fear of political Islam in contemporary French society. He calls for acknowledging the importance of the multicultural challenges to French society and the need for the republic to develop a better acceptance of migrants and their religious signs without stigmatizing or excluding them. The confinement of the analysis to the national scale stresses not only French singularity but also the role of the state. The public sphere is taken to be a given entity granted by French republicanism, not a secular space that is transformed and transgressed by Muslims. Bowen's analysis is in line with the politics of integration and accommodation of differences. In a way he argues that the potentialities of French singularity can also work for migrants, as they give up some of the troublesome differences of Islam to become part of the republic.

In her book on the politics of the veil, Joan W. Scott engages a more argumentative and critical approach in regard to the French notion of laïcité that works as an exclusionary force from the public sphere for Muslim migrants. She argues that the new version of French laïcité, hardened and framed in opposition to Islam, became "an ideological tool in an anti-Muslim campaign."[12] She criticizes the proponents of the headscarf ban in the schools, for whom "integration is a prerequisite for education," which is at odds with the French historical tradition that the school produces integration by means of the shared experience of education, where some commonality is created. In her view, banning headscarves in public schools makes the point clear that only one notion of personhood is possible and assimilation is the only route to membership in the nation. Thus, one cannot be both Muslim and French.[13] The notion of personhood includes that of womanhood as well in setting the model of citizenship. Scott acknowledges the realm of sexuality as a battleground between secular and Islamic conceptions of selfhood and points to the contradictions in Western feminism, which for her is caught up by a "psychology of denial." She addresses a criticism to the universal claims of French secularism and feminism that fail to open up a space for recognition of religious and cultural differences.

The expression "Secularism is not to be reduced to a piece

of cloth" was revealed to be false and true at the same time. False, because the debates on secularism became a matter of clothing, body, and gender. True, because by enacting a law, French society at large expressed its determination to maintain and reinforce the principles of republican secularism. But on the whole, the headscarf debate and the law signified a turning point for French secularism, leading to a critical review of its own understanding and self-presentation in its encounter with Islam. Islam became an active factor in redefining French self-presentation. By the same token, the defense of women's rights and gender equality were placed as core values of republican secularism. The debate also reconfigured the feminist field in France. The majority of French feminists defended the headscarf ban and aligned with republican values, while a minority stood up against the exclusion of girls from the schools, defending, for instance, the principle of "one school for all."[14] The novelty was that new faces of migrant women appeared in public, voicing the struggle of young secular Muslim women for gender equality and secularism against their own oppressive communities in the banlieues (the movement of "neither prostitute nor submissive" [ni putes ni soumises] is a case in point). In distinction from these "acceptable" voices of migrant women, a "subaltern" movement of French migrants emerged and took a critical stand against the republican legacy of secular feminism and the colonial past. They labeled themselves autochthones of the republic [les indigènes de la république]. Thus, the Islamic headscarf debate (although there was more consensus on what the core values of the republic are than debate) calls for rethinking secularism from a new perspective.[15]

The headscarf became a central marker in changing and re-shaping perceptions and definitions of secularism, feminism, and the colonial legacy in France.

The headscarf became such a powerful marker because it condensed in one single icon the multilayered realm of conflict around gender, space, and intercultural issues (and, more precisely, civilizational issues, to the extent that the cultural difference is external to the Western model of the Enlightenment). The symbol draws attention to a strong visual aspect of the Islamic religion, both in ways in which it is personalized and embodied and in ways it is communicated and perceived. The notion of *conspicuous* that is used in the wording of the French law illustrates the importance of the visual aspect and the intercultural discord in the creation of a public. The notion also conveys ambiguity in terms of intersubjective communication: where to draw the boundaries between a conspicuous and a discreet sign (for instance, crosses and the hands of Fatima are allowed if they are small enough, but Jewish yarmulkes and Sikh turbans are not)—that is, which religious signs and clothing are to be considered conspicuous, and according to whose gaze? A religious sign that is familiar to a given community and therefore invisible to their eye can become noticeable, conspicuous, and disturbing in the eyes of the members of a different religion. It is interesting to note here that the classrooms were secularized in France at the beginning of the twentieth century by what is known as the Jules Ferry laws; however, in Germany the presence of a Christian cross on classroom walls became an issue when it came to be visible in a multireligious migrant country.[16] The personal meanings attached to signs and clothing may differ from their public perceptions; similarly, public connotations of religious signs can impinge on self-perceptions. The ambiguities and discussions around the notion of *conspicuous* attest to the importance of the visual, symbolic, and communicative aspects in debating the different meanings and powers of the secular.

As an outcome of this confrontational encounter, both French secularism and the Islamic headscarf, in different ways, ceased to be a monocultural issue. The making of a law guaranteed that the Islamic headscarf is imprinted in the French collective memory; it became an intrinsic part of French history, a "French possession."[17] On the other hand, as the Islamic headscarf entered the public realm of European societies, it ceased to be an exclusively Muslim issue, limited to a Muslim-majority country or to a region. Thereby it signifies that European Muslims as a minority group living in a secular (and Christian) environment face a set of new issues (interfaith relations, modes of gender sociability, dietary habits, construction of mosques, use of cemeteries, and so on) that are not raised in a similar fashion, if at all, in national Muslim-majority contexts. Muslim migrants are called to (re)think about their religion and faith from the vantage point of their experiences as European citizens. Similarly, European secularism is refashioned in confrontation with issues raised by Muslims. Accounts of secularism limited to genealogies of the Christian religion and Christendom fall short of grasping the contemporary forms of intercultural interaction.

Turkish secularism hints at the ways in which the power of the secular works as part of a "civilizing mission" that operates at the level of everyday life practices and changes material culture, corporal appearances, spatial divisions, and gender sociability. Although Turkish secularism, laiklik, is mainly seen in its political and authoritarian aspects, it also provides us with one of the most resourceful historical examples of how the modern secular is indigenized and acted out in changing Muslim definitions of self, ethics, and aesthetics. The Kemalist reforms exemplify the formations of the secular Muslim, namely Muslim habitations and iterations of the secular in a noncolonial context that is characterized by voluntary and authoritarian adaptations of the secular.[18]

The gendered dimension of secularism has been an intrinsic feature of Turkish modernization from its very beginnings in the late Ottoman period, when different literary and political currents of thought were in favor of education of girls, free love, gender sociability, and the visibility of women in public against the religious and traditional morals of society, which, they thought, confined women to interior spaces and to established roles, imposing gender segregation and permitting polygamy. Turkish laiklik meant that the republican state had a strong will to endorse a public sphere where religion would be absent and women would be present. The reforms of the republic, whether they provided legal rights (with the abolition of Sharia law and the adoption of a civil family code), political rights (women's right to vote and eligibility), educational rights (coeducation),

88

or European clothing habits (taking off the veil, but also banning the fez, traditional headgear, for men), all underpinned the Turkish way of equating secularism and the "civilized" person, embodied by women's rights and visibility from the very beginning of the republic.

The powers of the secular can be traced in its capacity to develop a set of disciplinary practices, both corporal and spatial, that are inseparable from the formations of the secular self. Secularism is about state politics, lawmaking, and constitutional principles, but foremost it permeates and establishes the rhythm of a phenomenology of everyday life practices.[19] Secularism is not a "neutral," power-free space and a set of abstract principles; it is embodied in individuals' agencies and imaginaries. Turkish laiklik illustrates well the didactic aspect of secularism: secularism as a learning process, as inhabiting a new space and learning new body techniques, forms a habitus of a secular way of life (considered to be a higher form of life, because of its equation with Western civilization). Ernest Gellner has referred to Turkish secularism as a "didactic secularism" in the sense that it was imposed by state authoritarianism.[20] But it is also didactic in the sense that it becomes a learned practice, a habitus to be performed by new elites, men and women who owe their status to the republican schools (that is, secular elites have been formed by means of the state monopoly over the educational system and the adoption of the Latin script in 1928). Secularism designates a habitus in the sense that it is a set of performative techniques and discursive practices (including speaking and writing in modern Turkish, from which Arabic and Persian influences have been eliminated) that are learned and interiorized; it also designates a "colonized" life-world in the sense that it frames these realms in reference to Western notions of truth, ethics, and aesthetics.

The Turkish Republic created its own secular elites and its own secular spaces—schools, but also opera and ballet houses, concert halls, ballrooms (mainly in Ankara, the capital city, which seeks to distinguish itself from the cosmopolitan Istanbul), all the landmarks of a new way of life, women's visibility in public life, and social mixing of men and women. Learning how to inhabit these new spaces—husband and wife, walking hand in hand; man and woman shaking hands, dancing at balls, and dining together—characterizes acquiring a new habitus required by secular modernity. The modern secular life becomes a sign of prestige through its performative everyday practices, pictorial representations, and material culture.

The emergence of Islam in the post-1980 period addresses a challenge to the hegemonic control of the secular over public spaces and personal habitus. Muslim students' desire to wear headscarves on university campuses meant that the secular was transgressed by the gendered religious. The Turkish and French headscarf debates, in spite of the differences, have some commonalities to the extent that in both cases gender equality and secular spaces framed the debate. The ban, both in Turkey and France, revealed the unwritten secular laws and social imaginaries that governed the public spaces.[21] Spaces such as schools, universities, hospitals, swimming pools, and the Parliament became controversial once the secular rules had been broken by the transgression caused by religious signs and pious practices. The secular backdrop of the public sphere came to the forefront both in Turkey and in France. In both cases secularism endorsed a role of assimilation of Muslims into the Western life-world, a civilizing mission, and compulsory learning of the disciplinary practices of the secular in the public spaces. And in both cases religious visibility and femininity defied the hegemony of the secular over definitions of self, sexuality, and space.

Secular and Islamic: Spatial Transgressions

The threshold for the tolerable is framed differently in the French and Turkish contexts. When and how do religious signs cease to be discreet and acceptable and catch the eye, thus turning into a conspicuous sign that is troubling for public order? When does the headscarf cease to be perceived as a symbol of authentic faith and become a political symbol that provokes a public debate? The head covering of the peasant, the working-class migrant woman, or the grandmother is considered as a symbol of either faith or tradition and therefore is acceptable and invisible, whereas the young woman's headscarf at schools and universities unsettles the secular divisions between pious and traditional, public and modern, and becomes conspicuous—that is, visible to the public eye. It provokes powerful emotions of the secular, anger and aversion to the extent that the temporal comfort (religion as a relic from the past) and spatial separations (personal and public) between secular and religious disappear. Today's covered women, as compared with women in the past, who were segregated in private, are both pious and public. They become visible in leaving the traditional interior spaces reserved for women and entering public spaces such as schools, universities, and Parliament, namely the spaces reserved for the secular elite. Women's moves represent a spatial transgression for both the religious and the secular. Women who are proponents of the headscarf distance themselves from secular models of feminist emancipation but also seek autonomy from male interpretations of Islamic precepts. They represent a rupture of the frame both with secular female self-definitions and religious male prescriptions.[22] They want to have access to secular education, follow new life trajectories that are not in conformity with traditional gender roles, and yet fashion and assert a new pious self. The frontiers between the traditional and the pious are unsettled, as are those between the secular and the public.

The symbol of veiling needs to be readjusted, given its meanings in the past and its contemporary appropriations by new profiles of Muslim women. The symbol of veiling is undergoing a change to the extent that it is adopted by Muslim women who are overtly and assertively pious and public. The veiling is in the process of being changed from a sign of stigma and inferiority into a sign of empowerment,[23] in some cases by means of access to political power; a sign of distinction and prestige, by means of acquisition of social and cultural capital; and a sign of new aesthetics for Muslim women, by means of fashion production.[24] It is certainly a challenge to secular conceptions of female emancipation, but also to male Islam, which identifies the veil with submission to its own authority. But at the same time, the transformation of the veil from a symbol of faith, religion, and stigma into a sign of power, prestige, and aesthetics calls for a composition of the religious and secular divide in new ways.

One can depict this process in the Turkish context as the formation of Islamic counter-elites, which in many ways mirror the republican secular elites.[25] The making of the elites follows similar paths: access (especially for girls) to education (both secular and religious); the unveiling and reveiling of women; the disciplinary practices of the secular versus religious habitus; transgression of gender roles from the interior/private realm to the exterior/public domain. Muslim women cover their bodies yet become visible to the public eye, and hence unsettle the religious norms of modesty and the secular definitions of the feminist self. They are searching for ways to combine piousness and publicness, Muslim and modern at the same time (either by double assertion or by double negation), transforming the meanings of both.

Islam becomes a source of capital for the ascension of those social groups and social classes that were deprived of social and cultural recognition in the past. Their entry into the spaces reserved for the secular middle classes (universities, Parliament, and locations of leisure and consumption such as beaches, concert halls, and shopping malls) disturb the unwritten laws that exclude the religious. The arduous and long process of lifting the ban on the headscarf in Turkish universities and the French lawmaking process to ban the headscarf in the public schools both illustrate the passionate and visceral aspects of the secular imaginaries. Despite the fact that new legislation in Turkey to lift the ban on wearing the headscarf in the universities was formulated not in terms of freedom of religious faith but in the name of equal access of all to higher education and for preventing discrimination, and that it therefore was in conformity with

European norms and dress codes, it provoked fear and anger among secular women, the public, the media, and the establishment.[26] It was feared that ending the ban would provide a first step toward paving the way for the escalation of Muslim claims and the spread of the headscarf beyond the universities to public schools and Parliament and among public servants and professionals. The same fear of the escalation of Islamic claims and visibility from public schools to hospitals to public life in general was expressed in France. The Islamic visibilities in public provoked secular anxieties and mobilized feminist militancy.

The headscarf ban revealed the tacit secular norms and imaginaries of the public spaces that were taken for granted as the background picture.

In a similar fashion, public demonstrations in Turkey against the legislation to lift the headscarf ban signaled the transformation of Turkish secularism from state politics to street politics. The form of secularism that has been implemented as a principle of the republican state has been widely considered as a top-down ideology, foreign in its roots (inspired by French laïcité) and destined to disappear if not backed up by the army's power. But in the past three decades, secularism came to be expressed in women's groups and associations advocating the defense of a "modern secular way of life."[27] Public demonstrations during the summers of 2007 and 2008 involved millions and spread from one city to another. The abundance of national flags and the slogans that were widely used in these demonstrations signified the state-oriented and nationalist features of Turkish secularism. But they also meant a new secular protest movement in the streets. The secular formed a mise-en-scène by numbers, by masses getting together, by symbols (oversized flags acquiring a new popularity), by photographs and the sayings of Atatürk, but also by new modes of secular clothing for women (in tune with the colors of the Turkish flag: red and white miniskirts, ties, and caps), accompanied by music and slogans. Secularism was performed in public collectively and visually; the numbers mattered, to display that secularism was not in the hands of a minority; a new market of icons and clothing attempted to create a secular fashion; and the use of Atatürk's pictures, deeds, and words provided a frame for commemorating Turkish secularism.[28] In many similar ways secularism was mirroring and competing with Islam to create a repertoire of action. One can speak of a two-way transgression; while the religious broke the rules and moved into secular spaces of the republic, the secular descended from state to street politics.

In both France and Turkey, cultural confrontations and emotional tensions between secular and religious groups are unfolding in the realm of everyday life, involving a tacit process of mirroring and competing with each other. Both for the secular and for the religious, visual signs, gendered performances, and spatial divisions become the battleground for self-distinction and discipline.

European Secularity and Islamic Self

The powers of both secularism and Islam cease to be bound to given national formations or distinctive civilizations but become part of a cross-civilizational and transnational European public. On one hand, the European public sphere cannot be thought of as a national public written large; genealogical, historical readings of its formation do not capture the present-day encounters between different language communities, cultural codes, ethnicities, and religions. On the other hand, readings of Islam confined to the national politics of migration or, in an opposite move, linked to global jihadist movements do not take into account the ways in which Islam becomes European.

The negative aspects of geographical and cultural displacements are often highlighted in the case of migration and the politicization of Islam. Conditions of migration are depicted in terms of economic precariousness, cultural alienation, and personal frustration caused by deficiencies of integration, leading to insular communities, particularly ghetto-like suburbs, that appear to nurture insecurity and the political radicalization of Islam. Islam is under the impact of dynamics of social mobility and modernity to the extent that it is no longer exclusively a reference for groups who are attached to a place, to a territory, and to traditions. Olivier Roy points to the "de-territorialization" of Muslims, those who follow a global trajectory in their strategies and formations of neofundamentalism.[29] There is another aspect of social mobility that is often neglected in approaches to Islam yet is crucial to understanding the formation of new Muslim subjectivities. Social mobility is not merely about deracinating and alienating; it is also about reterritorialization, opening up a space for the elaboration of improvisations, adaptations, and inventions of subjectivities and a sense of belonging. Concomitant with the move into modern life spaces, religion and traditions cease to be prearranged entities; Islam no longer appears as a norm that is taken for granted, transmitted from one generation to another, socially embedded and institutionalized, but, on the contrary, faces discontinuities in its transmission and claims of authority. Islam, a binding force among those who belonged to a locality, to a particular confession, and to a nation-state, becomes a reference going beyond the local frontiers, providing an imaginary bond between Muslims, and enabling Muslim self-fashioning.

We can speak of Islam as providing the mechanisms of discipline, restraint, and empowerment for a new self-fashioning of Muslims; they adapt and improvise their faith under new conditions of social mobility and cultural displacement. There is an element of invention (of traditions) in the self-fashioning process that is not separated from disciplinary practices of self-restraint (control of sexuality, mind, and self). The notion of self-fashioning helps us move beyond the category of identity that remains equated with authenticity and emancipation. The notion of self-fashioning is also helpful in conveying the visual and corporal aspects of personal identity; additionally, self-fashioning resonates with the disciplinary powers of both the secular and the religious idioms. The headscarf expresses the self-fashioning of Muslim girls with disciplinary categories of Islam, but for them faith is not a prearranged category and enters into the domain of improvisation, adaptation, and invention. It is a sign of self-restraint (hijab means modest behavior and dress) and self-fashioning, including, in literal terms, the production of Islamic fashion.

The faith cannot be taken for granted, as if the Islamic faith were carried in the luggage of the migrants as they arrive from villages and small towns in their home countries. Social mobility, on the contrary, means distancing oneself from one's country of origin and living under conditions of displacement in which the ties with the traditional, institutional forms of religiosity are cut off. Social groups that are undergoing social mobility are those that distance themselves from the family background, local authorities, and institutionalized traditions in which Islam was a prearranged norm. Contemporary piety is being established not as a once-and-for-all category, handed down from one generation to another or carried from the hometown, but in movement, in improvisation, and in acquisition through religious knowledge and self-fashioning.

In contexts of migration, Islam becomes part of an "intellectual learning" endeavor rather than learning by recitation and imitation from previous generations. Contemporary actors of Islam very often make the distinction between those who are Muslim by tradition and those who are Muslim by education, valorizing the second. Acquiring religious knowledge means learning how to read and interpret the Quran, achieving fluency in the Arabic language, but also engaging in collective prayers and conversations to enhance the sense of belonging to a community of believers (umma). The acquisition of Islamic knowledge combines religious norms of virtue and disciplinary practices of body; praying, dietary habits, and sexual modesty become practices that require continuous surveillance and rigorous application in a secular environment.[30] Learning Islam by attending seminars and youth institutions but also by means of performative practices requires an alternative space—an alternative to both secular hegemonic and traditional religious "counterpublics."[31] Pious Muslims have to deal on an everyday basis with the incongruities between their faith and their secular public lives. In a Muslim-minority context, everything that is considered natural—for instance, the ritual of the ablution before prayer—necessitates a particular reserved space, and the purification ritual becomes a complicated matter in its absence and disturbing in its visibility in public restrooms. Similarly, praying five times a day in a society organized according to secular time and in working spaces with instrumental rationality brings forth the question of praying rooms; use of secular spaces for religious observance will also bring conspicuous, disturbing visibility. While praying, a Muslim woman covers her hair; if she does so in a workplace, she becomes instantly visible, recognizable as a Muslim. There are therefore strategies for visibility as well as for dissimulation of faith. The Islamic covering is one distinctive representation of piety that creates immediate recognition for male and female citizens. There are, for instance, pious Muslim women who do not adopt the veil but for whom the relation to a secular way of life—modes of address with non-Muslim men, dating, and alcohol consumption— becomes fuzzy in the absence of a clear-cut frontier, a visible religious marker.[32]

The public sphere becomes the site where the importance of the visual is played out. Especially where issues of Islamic religion and gender are in question, the gaze and spatial conventions acquire a greater salience in mediating power relations. When Muslim women cross the borders between inside and outside, the arousal of multiple senses—sight, smell, touch, and voice—and desires requires the preservation of decency and control of public morality. The visibility of Muslim women in public life means crossing and transgressing the interior, intimate, secret, gendered space, forbidden to foreign males' gaze (*mahrem*). Veiling suggests the importance of the ocular (avoiding the gaze, casting down one's eyes). The notion of sexual modesty (*edep*) underpins the Muslim self-fashioning. Such Islamic behavior—the aesthetics of edep, the valorization of the mahrem with retained body exposure and self-protection, controlled gender sociability, and gender-differentiated modes of address—enact ways of being Muslim in secular publics. These behaviors are not alien to Muslim memory and culture. They are rooted in past traditions and collective memory as well as in the religious habitus. But they are not simple conventions that have always been there and that are unconsciously handed down from one generation to another. The habitus provides, in Pierre Bourdieu's terms, a source of improvisations; it allows for a process of continual correction and adjustment.[33] Islamic public performances reinvent religious traditions, correct and improvise them in counterdistinction to secular norms and disciplinary practices.

We can speak of what Victor Turner calls "performative reflexivity," as a "condition in which a sociocultural group, or its most perceptive members, acting representatively, turn, bend, or reflect back upon themselves, upon the relations, actions, symbols, meanings, and codes, roles, statuses, social structures, ethical and legal rules, and other sociocultural components which make up their public 'selves.'"[34] Islamic performance has a reflexive character to the extent that the codes and symbols embedded in the religious culture are critically appropriated and distanced from the traditional culture. It also has a reflexive feature in being engaged with a series of issues that are raised when one is a Muslim in a secular and Christian-majority society, ranging from spaces for practicing faith to public modes of self-presentation, sociability of men and women to competition with secular definitions of emancipation and femininity. Muslims enter into common spaces of everyday life experience with Europeans that in turn call for mutual transformations and reflexivity—a reflexivity that is translated not only in discursive terms but also in the transformation of the material culture.

One can suggest that European Islam is following similar dynamics to what Charles Taylor calls the post-Durkheimian situation, in which faith is not connected, or is only weakly connected, to a national political identity.[35] But as Taylor argues, the human aspiration to religion does not disappear, and does not become a trivialized and utterly privatized spirituality. Similarly, Islam offers a sense of "believing," yet without "belonging" either to a national community or to an institutionalized religion. Islam becomes personally pious and publicly visible, disembedded from its institutionalized forms but more voluntary and mental; it is learned, performed, and imagined socially. Hence Islam is shaped by the secular age. According to Taylor, religious and antireligious people in modernity have more assumptions in common than they often realize. He argues that in the modern age, religious experience becomes part of *expressive individualism*, that is, finding one's own way against a model imposed from outside—be it from society, the previous generation, or religious authority.[36] But in distinction from the *expressive revolution*, in which the ethic of authenticity is ac-

companied by a sexual revolution and undercuts the close connections of religious faith with a certain sexual morality, Islamic
expressive individualism brings forth alternative notions of self,
morality, and piousness. That is why the discord with Islam is
carried at the forefront by the secular French feminists, by those
who are committed to the imperatives of the expressive revolution and sexual revolution, the cultural legacies of the 1968
movement. The Islamic presence in Europe defies the secular
norms of individuality, gender equality, and sexuality. Monocivilizational readings of both the secular and the religious fail to
account for this ongoing process of mutual transformation.

5   The Gendered Nature of the Public Sphere

n this chapter I focus on the gendered nature of the public sphere that underpins secular modernization projects in Muslim-majority countries. In Muslim contexts of modernity the boundaries of the public sphere are (re)shaped by the centrality of women's visibility in their bodies and in their words and agencies. In other words, "women's visibility, women's mobility and women's voices"[1] constitute the political stakes around which the public sphere is defined. In order to study the intricate nature of connections between gender, politics, and the public sphere, I highlight two historical moments of change in Turkish history and contemporary experience. One refers to the projects of modernization in the 1920s, the second to the movements of Islamization in the 1980s. A similar historical classification concerning projects of modernism on the one hand and Islamism on the other, as well as the centrality of the question of gender in shaping political debates, social transformations, and definitions of public and private spheres, can be extended to other Muslim contexts of modernities. Historically, however, since it defined women as public citizens, the Turkish mode of modernization can be considered the most radical engagement among Muslim countries. Equating national progress with women's emancipation defined the backbone of Kemalist feminism. On the other hand, during the last two decades, Turkey, like other Muslim countries, has witnessed the advent of Islamism.

I refer to Islamism as a contemporary social movement that takes varying political forms in varying national contexts; it led to a revolution in Iran, came to power by democratic means in Turkey, or engendered clandestine terrorist networks. The common features among them include the urban nature of the phenomenon, the participation of the young urban-educated youth (both male and female), and, at the ideological level, the criticism of traditional interpretations of Islam and the quest for an Islamic alternative to modernity. It is a sociocultural movement in the sense that it redefines an Islamic collective identity and enters into a conflict about the orientation of the cultural model.[2] In speaking of Islamism, I differentiate therefore between *Muslim*, which expresses religious faith, and *Islamist*, which refers to a social movement through which Muslim faith is turned into a collective identity as a basis for an alternative social and political project. Thus Islamism implies a critique and even a discontinuity with the given categories of Muslim identity; it is an attempt to rename and reconstruct Muslim identity by freeing it from traditional interpretations and by challenging assimilative forces of secular modernity.

Islamism's most visible and challenging symbol is "the veiling issue,"[3] sometimes referred to as the "headscarf dispute," that is to say, the demand by Muslim girls to be allowed to cover their heads according to Islamic precepts while attending public schools. The public debate on Islamism became more relevant in relation to gender issues especially in post-1980 Turkey. The restoration of political life after the 1980 coup d'état and the privatization of television and radio brought forth heated public debates. The public sphere gained relative autonomy from the state ideology and the roundtables, panels, and talk shows provided a very popular medium for intellectuals, political actors, and citizens from both religious and secular, right and left worldviews, discussing the issues of secularism and democracy. The Islamist Welfare Party (Refah Partisi) became the senior member of a coalition government in July 1996 and exacerbated the debates on the place of Islam in politics. Suspected of having an Islamist agenda, it was forced out of power by the Turkish military backed up by the secular establishment on February 28, 1997. This "post-modern coup" did not, however, prevent the coming to power of a new party, AKP (Justice and Development Party), founded by a young generation of Islamists with the leadership of Recep Tayyip Erdoğan in 2002. The veiling issue was so salient that it took a decade for AKP to lift the ban on wearing the headscarf in universities.

Women's issues are pivotal in the shaping of modern political debate and the public sphere in Muslim countries. Two broader implicit preoccupations underlie this emphasis on the connections between gender and the public sphere. The first is related to the phenomenon of contemporary Islamism and the related questions of democracy. Political scientists explained Islamist movements as a political strategy for the implementation of a state governed by Islamic law, that is to say, as fundamentalist movements trying to implement Sharia law. They explain Islamic radicalism merely by economic deprivations and political frustrations. In such approaches, the religion is instrumentalized for political means and the question of women is secondary. At the other extreme, the feminist and anthropological approaches focused on questions of religion and women's identity, dismissing the transformative forces of gender and Islam in contemporary politics.[4] We should refocus our analyses at the crossroads of politics, gender power relations and the public sphere. Only in recentering the question of women can we gain a better grasp of the nature of the discord between Islamists and secularists. In other words, gender issues, such as communitarian morality, women's modesty, and the social segregation between men and women, are central in understanding the display of Islamist politics in redefining the boundaries between the intimate and the public sphere. I argue that, in Islamist politics, the stakes of democracy are inseparable from the (shrinking or expanding) boundaries of the public sphere, which in turn are determined foremost by categories of morality, identity, and thus gender issues. In short, politics of intimacy and public visibility of Islam are interrelated.

The second set of implicit preoccupations of this chapter is related to the specific nature of non-Western modernities, that is to say, the ways in which modernity is (re)appropriated in Muslim contexts. This requires attention to asymmetrical trajectories in the emergence of the public sphere in different contexts. Whereas in Western European history the public sphere emerged as a liberal-bourgeois sphere, with women (and the working class) initially excluded and thus also excluded from the definition of the universal citizen,[5] in the Turkish mode of modernization, women's visibility and citizenship rights endorsed the existence of the public sphere. But by the same token, the public sphere, as a site of the modernist project, was tightly monitored by the secular elites. Consequently, in Muslim contexts of modernity, the public sphere does not emerge as an outcome of a liberal bourgeois ideology but of authoritarian state modernism. Hence the gendered and the authoritarian nature of the public sphere in the shaping of secularist elites and modernist projects in Muslim countries define the particular aspect of non-Western appropriations of modernity.

The Public Sphere as a Secular Way of Life

The Turkish case of secularism was distinguished by its radicality among the Muslim majority countries. The Turkish Republic was proclaimed in 1923. By a series of so-called Kemalist revolutions, first the Caliphate was abolished in 1924, and then family law was completely secularized (a unique experience among Muslim countries) by the adoption of the Swiss Civil Code in 1926 (hence religious marriages and polygamy were forbidden); finally, the Turkish Republic was declared a secular state by a constitutional amendment in 1937.

Although Turkish secularism was inspired by the French laïcité, which is basically shaped by the gradual separation of state affairs from religion, the neutrality of the state toward various denominational groups, and the irreligiosity of the public sphere, it followed a different pattern.[6] First of all, for instance, Turkish secularism does not encourage the separation and autonomy of religion from state power. On the contrary, institutional religion is brought under total state control in order to bring the religious idiom and education in line with the modernist and rationalist ideal. Second, it is hard to speak of the state's equidistance from all denominational groups, because Sunni Islam implicitly represents state religion, which is challenged today by the Alevis, a religious minority of Shia origin.[7] Only in regard to the third feature, the irreligiosity of the public sphere, can we speak of similarities. The similarity between the two cases, French and Turkish, lies in their secularist and universalistic conception of the public sphere; that is, one enters into public spaces, mainly into the realms of education and politics, leaving behind one's particularistic identities and religious affiliations. Consequently it is the universalistic conception of citizenship regardless of gender, religion, and ethnicity that underlies the secularism of the public sphere in accordance with the ideals of the Enlightenment.[8] The secularization of the public space, the disappearance of religious symbols and practices (such as the removal of the crucifix from schools and courts), is a significant aspect of French secularism. But this process took place gradually and through political democratization during France's Third Republic.[9] In contrast, in Turkey, as in other Muslim countries, secularism as a prerequisite of Westernization was implemented by authoritarian political systems.

The secularist project that was shaped during the single-party period of the Turkish Republic meant the expunging of all religious signs and practices from the public sphere in order to install the "modern way of life"; the banning of religious shrines (*türbe*) and the dervish orders (*tarikat*) (1925); the prohibition of traditional Ottoman headgear, the red felt cap, the fez, and its replacement with the European hat (1925); the adoption of the Western calendar (1926); the replacement of Arabic script with Latin script (1928); imposition of certain types of music (Western classical music for instance) at state radio stations and television channels—all reflect the desire to cut the links with the Islamic world and turn toward the Western, read "civilized," world. Ernest Gellner calls Kemalist secularism a "didactic secularism":[10] it is moralistic and pedagogical; it imposes and teaches secularism as a Western way of living. The secularization of education, politics, and also of everyday life practices and of social spaces was crucial to the Turkish modernist project. The adoption of the metric system, the Gregorian calendar, the celebration of the New Year, the acceptance of Sunday as the official day of rest, and the civil ceremony in marriage are all examples of the imposition of Western secularism at the level of organization of time, daily life, and social practices. In other words, the public sphere denotes a space for the making of the new republican elites, while it excludes the others, namely those who do not conform to this "new life," that is, the non-Westernized, observant Muslim populations. The public sphere does not initially appear as a democratic space providing equal access of all citizens to a rational-critical debate on public issues, but it emerges as a stage on which modernist patterns of conduct and living are performed.

Further, in a Muslim context, the existence of a public sphere is attested by women's visibility and social mixing of men and women. It is the construction of women as public citizens and women's rights (even more cherished than the construction of citizenship and civil rights) that are the backbones of Turkish modernism. The removal of the veil, the establishment of compulsory coeducation, civil rights for women including eligibility to vote and to hold office, and the abolition of Islamic family law guaranteed the public visibility and citizenship of women. In other words, women's bodily, social, and political visibility defined the modernist public sphere in the Kemalist project. The Turkish Kemalist project of modernity cannot be grasped without understanding the centrality of women both as agents and symbols of secular modernism. Each revolution redefines the attributes of an "ideal man"; yet Kemalist revolution represents and idealizes new women figures in their social roles, public visibility, Western appearances, and ways of life.

The celebration and acquisition of women's visibility both in their corporeality and in their public roles as models of emulation furthered the secularization of public life. Photographs of unveiled women, women in athletic competitions, women pilots, women professionals, and photographs of men and women living European lifestyles depicted the new modernist representations of a "prestigious" life.[11] Turkish novels written in the early republican era would base their cast on this new "civilized" way of life, take its decor, goods, and clothing as their backdrop, celebrate the ideal attributes and rituals of a "progressive and civilized" republican individual: tea-salons, dinners, balls, and streets would be the public spaces for the socializing of sexes; husband and wife walking hand-in-hand, man and woman shaking hands, dancing at balls, and dining together would characterize the European style of gender relations. Among the cast of characters would appear serious, working women devoted to national progress—these to be distinguished from "superficial" and mannered claims to Europeanness.[12] Against Ottoman cosmopolitanism, Kemalist women characters, affirming seriousness, modesty, and devotion, would accommodate the presumed pre-Islamic Anatolian culture and thereby incarnate the nationalist project.

Yakup Kadri Karaosmanoğlu's novel, *Ankara*, published in 1934, is among the best examples of attempts to overcome the tensions between Western cosmopolitanism and nationalist modernism by accommodating a woman's public participation with the values of modesty. The leading female character in the novel, Selma, originally from Istanbul, is depicted positively as a "Westernized" woman who is alienated from her people and can find fulfillment only in being closer to people. Consequently, she moves from Istanbul to Ankara, the new capital of the republic since 1924, searching for "authentic" Anatolian roots for the nationalist project, distinct from Istanbul, the site of Ottoman cosmopolitanism. Selma is portrayed with sympathy as having high esteem among the vigorous neighborhood women, as a "boyish person" without "hips and breasts" (physical traits considered European), and leading a "modern" way of life, that is, eating at the same table with men and riding horses in their company. Nonetheless, the Western way of life, especially the one promoted by the cosmopolitan Istanbul elites and symbolized by the gramophone, Swiss governesses, white gloves, dancing, and bridge parties, is criticized by the novelist as a source of the leading female character's alienation not only from her own people but also from herself. Karaosmanoğlu calls on his characters to turn back to the "plain, intimate and strongly personal, sincere life" experienced during the period of the struggle for national independence. "Turkish women have forsaken their charshafs and veils to be able to work with more ease and comfort . . . Yes, Turkish women have claimed their freedom and used it not to dance, and to polish her nails . . . to be a puppet, but to undertake a demanding and serious role in the constitution and development of a new Turkey."[13] Hence women were paramount to the project of nationalist modernism and Westernized secularism. Republican men called on women to be active agents in the building of a modern nation. The emancipation of women from traditional and religious roles was desirable to the extent that women acquired public roles, public visibility for the national cause, which in turn implied collective consciousness and modesty rather than individualism.[14]

Women's participation in public life as citizens and as civil servants, their visibility in urban spaces, and their socialization with men all defined the modern secular way of life and indicated a radical shift from the social organization and gender roles framed by Islamic religion. In other words, in a Muslim context, secularism denotes a modern way of life, calling for the "emancipation" of women from religion, signified by veiling and the segregation of the sexes. Women as place-markers of social organization, interior and exterior definitions, private and public spheres, relate to the making of the modern individual, to the modern way of being.

Images of Kemalist women carry modernist aspirations for the public as well as for the domestic sphere. Women as public servants (at the service of the interests of the republican state), teachers (educative role), participating in beauty contests and sports festivals (emancipated in their bodies), performing on the stage (not fettered with religious prohibitions), going to restaurants, driving cars (occupying urban spaces)—all these new roles calling for public visibility were endorsed by the feminine elites and encouraged by the "paternalizing males"[15] of the young republic with a shared nationalistic pride in creating a new part of the "civilized" Western world. Domestic life and ideals were also under the influence of Western values, with a new emphasis on the bourgeois model of nuclear family and a new interest in health and hygiene.[16] New periodicals, advertisements, and novels brought domestic life under the public gaze or, in other words, modern domestic life was publicized. Women as modern homemakers, consumers of new hygienic products, and agents of child-rearing embodied the pedagogical civilizing mission in matters of modern living. The house and the domestic interior followed Westernized aspirations for the nuclear family and found their expression in the "comfortable, simple and plain cubic" architecture (Le Corbusier's ideas were a source of inspiration for a whole generation of Turkish architects throughout the 1930s).[17] The modernist project aimed to constitute a new way of being and living, transmitted primarily by women and their changing intimacies with men in a newly constituted public sphere.

Hence, in a modernizing project, the public sphere is closely monitored by the Turkish state: rigidly in the early republican years, especially during the single-party period from 1923 to 1946, softening gradually from the 1950s on with the transition to pluralistic democracy (a process interrupted by the military interventions of 1960, 1971, and 1980). During the post-1983 period, the public sphere gained more autonomy from the state and became the locus of all the competing movements of civil society (such as Islamist, Kurdish, Alevite, liberal) challenging the national, secularist, and homogeneous character of the republican project of the public sphere. The demand by female Muslim students to be allowed to attend university classes in their Islamic outfit constituted the most visible assault on this project and was perceived by the secular elites as an invasion of "their" public sphere (university classes, Parliament, television, concert halls, streets, etc.).

Veiling between Public Visibility and Communitarian Morality

Ironically, in a similar yet reversed way, women also played a central role in contemporary Islamist movements of the post-1980 period. The veiling of women became the most visible emblem and indicator of the Islamization of politics, male and female relations, reorganization of urban spaces, and daily practices. Between modernism and Islamism, the stakes remain the same; that is to say, the battlegrounds in each case continue to be the self-definitions, gendered spatial restructurings and practices, as well as civilizational affiliations. Women's agency and public visibility characterize contemporary Islamism and bring forth at the same time a challenge to traditional precepts of Islam calling for the seclusion and segregation of women. New actresses of Islamism make their way to public university education, to political life, and to the urban heterosocial spaces of modernity. Hence there is a kind of continuation and at the same time a reversal of modernist women's mode of participation in public life. In both cases, new public roles of women are acquired by access to education and justified by political society-building projects; both modernism and Islamism value women as educators and missionaries. Furthermore, women, in their differing semiologies of body, symbolize and publicly endorse the civilizational choices. Thus women are not secondary, auxiliary actors, but on the contrary significant signifiers for both the movement of modernism as well as that of Islamism. However, women's identities, whether seen in individual aspirations or collective feminist consciousness, are confined within the broader boundaries of political projects. Both images of women, the modernist and the Islamist, subordinate female identities, whether relating to individual or collective consciousness, to values of modesty demanded by the populist nature of both ideologies. Yet there is a shift in the image of the ideal woman from "modern yet modest" to "Islamic thus modest."[18] Islamist veiling expresses the unapologetic assertion of modesty and religiosity in new self-definitions of Muslim women.

It is this unapologetic stand toward modernity that distinguishes the identity-politics of contemporary Islamism.[19] Definitions of self, disputes on lifestyles and artistic expression, in short, body-politics and more specifically gender-politics, become a central stake in the public debate in which secularists oppose Islamists.

The coming to power of the Islamist Refah Party at the municipal level (on March 27, 1994) and as the senior partner of a coalition government (July 1996) brought to the surface these issues on the Turkish political agenda, problematizing the existing boundaries between the public and the private. Islamist politics aims for the moral control of the public sphere through such well-known actions as control over women's modesty by veiling, limiting the public encounter between the sexes, the prohibition of alcohol consumption, and censorship of the arts. Almost mirroring the stance of modernism, Islamic faith posits itself as a reference point for the reideologizing of seemingly trivial social issues of ways of living, speaking, relating to each other. All its expressions criticize the secular way of life and exhibit a desire to control the public sphere according to the requirements of an Islamic way of life. Control over women's sexuality and the regulation of social encounters between male and female citizens constitute a central issue in the moralization of the public sphere. Consequently, in a Muslim context, the dispute over lifestyles, far from being a trivial issue of individual choices or changing trends, defines the shrinkage or expansion of the boundaries of the public sphere, which in turn defines the stakes of democracy.

In other words, contemporary actors of Islamism have access to modern education, to urban life, and to politics, and they gain public visibility but refuse assimilation to the values of secularism and modernist elites. The reasons for Islamist radicalism are thus related to this quest for authenticity, to the class relations of domination and exclusion, and more precisely to the conflictual relations with modernist elites and their civilizational affiliations. It is important to note that the alteration in lifestyles, in aesthetic and ethical values that generated a civilizational shift from the Islamic to the Western, is not independent of class relations of power. Western taste as a social indicator of distinction established new social divisions, created new social status groups, and thus changed the terms of social stratification. Thus, there emerges a power struggle, *habitus* in Bourdieu's terms, beyond our language and will, encompassing habits of eating, body language, taste, and so forth.[20] Contemporary Islamic radicalism problematizes the Westernized habitus as a legitimation for elites and reveals this power struggle in an aggravated form.[21] It criticizes the equation of the civilized with the Westernized. As an alternative, it advances the Islamization of life and lifestyles.

The politicization of Islam empowers and promotes the return of Muslim actors, ethics, and aesthetics to the historical scene. In this respect, Islamist movements share with other contemporary Western social movements the same critical sensitivity regarding Enlightenment modernity. They are similar to feminist as well as civil rights, environmental, and ethnic movements in that all display the force of the repressed (religion, gender, nature, and ethnicity respectively) and all recapitulate the lost memories and identity-politics. Like feminism, which questions the universalistic and egalitarian claims of the category of human being and asserts instead the difference of women, Islamism problematizes the universalistic claims of Western civilization, which excludes Islamic difference. In other words, just as radical feminism refuses strategies to assimilate women in the category of human beings equated with attributes of male being and forges instead women's identity in terms of its difference, Islamism refuses strategies of assimilation in a modern civilization equated with Western culture and forges instead its own difference. In both cases, it is the refusal of assimilation and the unapologetic attitude toward egalitarian, monistic, and global forces of modernity that underpin the exacerbation of differences and identities. The motto "black is beautiful" is endemic for all new protest movements including Islamism, since they all reject assimilation to *men*, *white*, and *Western* and define their identity, their source of empowerment, and identity-politics in terms of *difference* as women, blacks, or Muslims. Similarly, the motto "Islam is beautiful" gains credence in Islamic contexts. The Islamic dress codes, ways of living, and modes of manifesting faith in public—all considered signs of backwardness, uncivilized ways, the dark side of modernity, forces of obscurantism, and thus taken to be signs responsible for Muslim oppression and exclusion—are reappropriated and accentuated by Islamist actors. Hence, through the political radicalization of Islam, Muslim identity becomes visible and seeks to acquire legitimacy in the modern political idiom. Islamism is the exacerbation of Muslim identity and its reconstruction in and by the modern world. In other words, Islamism renders Muslim actors visible in the public sphere by their exacerbated differences. And once again, the covering of women conveys the equivocal meanings and tensions between limitations of the self (modesty) and collective empowerment (difference), between public visibility and private intimacies.

The similarities to and contrasts with the Western feminist movement can provide us with some further clues for comprehending these paradoxes engendered by contemporary Islamism in relation to democracy and the public sphere. Both feminism and Islamism introduce the intimate, private realm, be it religion or sexuality, into politics. The motto of the feminist movement "the personal is political" contributed to the enlargement of politics toward issues of self-definition and male-female relations of domination. In a way, the feminist movement followed the drive of modern societies, which according to Michel Foucault, is to search for "truth" and (stemming from earlier Christian religious practices) to "confess" the most intimate experiences, desires, illnesses, uneasiness, and guilt in public.[22] This explains how everything considered to be the most difficult to say, everything forbidden, rooted in the personal and private spheres, becomes, once confessed, public, political, and changeable. Feminism (as shown by the novelty of its labels: abortion rights, sexual harassment, and date rape) contributes to this movement of exposure to and transparency in the public sphere, but equally to the broadening of democracy, which transforms intimate relations of domination into political relations of power.

With the advent of Islamist movements, faith, self-definitions, and male-female relations—all of which are aspects that concern intimate, private relations—are also brought to public light, into politics. But at the same time, this realm reappears as a site of religious identity's resistance against the assimilative power of Western secularism and modernity. In other terms, Islamism makes the interior-intimate gendered space a public issue, yet by the same token calls for political intervention to enforce women's modesty and its own models of male-female relations. Islamism tends to reinforce communitarian morality by redefining the public order in conformity with Islamic prohibitions.

Islamism finds an echo in non-Western contexts, due to

the awakening of the latent communitarian morality common to the recently urbanized social groups that feel insecure and threatened by the globalization of modernist values as transmitted by tourism, satellite TV, and consumer goods. Communitarian morality can be thought of as a trait of societies in which modern individualism, individual conscience, confession, and public exposure of the self were not endowed with the dominant role in the structuring of individual and society relations. In the West, one can recall that the modern individual emerges with the basic presupposition that absolute truth is a matter of individual conscience (implying private thoughts, self-accusation, and self-awareness)[23] and not that of collectivity. The Muslim context directs the individual to give oneself up to God and let the community (*cemaat*) guide one through life. Thus, communitarian guidance in moral affairs is legitimated by religion and by daily life practices, which can in turn articulate themselves in forms of authoritarianism from below. Contemporary Islamism reactivates communitarian morality in legitimizing and reshaping it with a political-religious idiom and agency. In this respect, the Salman Rushdie case—in which Muslim outrage went beyond the political manipulation from above of the death-fatwa by the Ayatollah Khomeini, swelling up from below as well—exemplifies the connections between communitarian values of morality and the conflict with the West over identity, as revived by contemporary radical Islamism. In a similar way, the interdependence between the Muslim community's fabric and religiosity and woman's morality is further revealed by an Egyptian case of blasphemy, less globalized than the Rushdie affair, yet more significant.[24] Dr. Nasr Abou Zeid, a professor of the University of Cairo working on the interpretations of the Quran, was accused of opposing the religious law, Sharia, and was consequently declared an apostate. In May 1993, Islamist lawyers arguing that a Muslim woman does not have the right to remain married with a non-Muslim, sued for Professor Zeid's divorce based on a religious law *hisba* (last applied in the 1950s, it gives every Muslim the right to bring charges against someone if he or she considers the overriding interests of the community to be threatened). This case reveals that the Islamization of public debate and the public sphere is not independent of women's role, women's modesty, chastity, and religiosity, all considered pillars of the integrity of the (lost) Muslim community. In a sense, contemporary Islamism can be read as an endeavor to recuperate the lost community. The restoration of certain signs, especially the (re)veiling of women, symbolizes this imagined political community in the sense that it reinforces the social ties among individuals who do not know each other but dream of broad and profound attachment.[25] Even more than as a political ideology, Islamism appears as an imagined community forged and reinforced by and within the realm of the sacred.[26]

On the one hand, the current veiling movements carry images of educated, urbanized, and militant Muslim women to the public sphere and render them visible in their political agency, while on the other hand recalling women's modesty and role as guardians of the communitarian morality, reinforcing the idea of the forbidden sphere. Women thus acquire legitimacy and visibility through their participation in higher education and Islamic politics. Yet there is a covert tension, a paradox in this mode of empowerment through Islamism. When women quit traditional life-cycles, thus making their personal life a matter of choice (for professional and/or political career) they also acquiesce in incarnating the Islamic way of life, Islamic morality, and Islamic community. Thus Islamism unintentionally engenders the individuation of women while simultaneously restraining it. Islamism allows women access to public life, but this is an access limited to the purported good of the community, to the missionary goal. The politicization of the Islamic way of life can be a hindrance for individual choices of lifestyles. And once again, the monitoring of the public sphere depends on the monitoring of women.

Yet human agency always has unintended consequences; the dynamics of action elude the intentions and wills of the actors themselves. Islamism is no exception to this rule. As it makes its way to the public sphere, it engenders new Muslim subjectivities, which in turn challenge the Islamist ideal of a homogeneous public order legitimated by a communitarian conscience.

The Homogeneity of the Public Sphere and the Emergence of Muslim Subjectivities

In the last two decades, especially with the advent of contemporary Islamist movements, the homogeneity of the secular public sphere in Turkey is undergoing a radical challenge. Islamist movements aim politically for the moral control of the public sphere, thereby restricting democracy; they also occupy and expand the public sphere, creating new Islamic public visibilities and new Islamic public spaces. The bastions of modernity, such as the university campuses, the media, and politics, until recently exclusive domains of the secular elites in Turkey, are increasingly witnessing the "intrusion" of Islamist actors. A new figure, that of the Islamist public intellectual, whose modern university education provides access to secular as well as Islamic sources of knowledge, and who can be a journalist, politician, or academician, a man or a woman, competes with secular elites for cultural, political, and media power. Not without difficulty, friction, and hostility, secular elites are sharing university classes, academic conferences, public roundtables, talk shows, seats in Parliament, municipalities, concert halls, and boat-trips on the Bosphorus with new Muslim public faces. The latter compete for an audience in electoral politics but also for a share of the commercial market, for media ratings, and for followers in literate culture.

Therefore, the emergence of the Islamic public sphere enters into a very complex, competitive, equivocal relationship with modernity; it cannot be reduced to the identity politics of resistance to modernism and consumerism. The relationships between "markets and freedom, commodity and identity, property and pleasure" are far more complex and decisive in the construction of the public spheres.[27] For instance, the black public sphere in the United States "uses performativity to capture audiences" calling on the "black community" to buy this or read that "because it is authentically Black."[28] In a similar way, Islamism carves a space for itself, ranging from products of cultural criticism such as Islamic novels, films, music, and newspapers through alternative consumption patterns, such as Islamic outfit and fashion shows, to the Islamization of urban ways of living, such as restaurants and hotels that respect Islamic rules demanding nonalcoholic beverages and the observance of prayer hours.

The recently acquired visibility of Islam in the public sphere competes and conflicts with the secularist points of view but also provokes tensions within Islamist politics. The politicization of Islam renders publicly visible new issues and new actors, but radical Islamism calls for modesty and censorship in the public presentation of self. It carries new actors to public visibility, providing them with a new realm of opportunities ranging from cultural mediation through professional politics and journalism to consumption, yet it tries to constrain and confine this realm within ideological boundaries. Hence there is an inbred tension between individuation strategies, self-definitions, and subjectivities of Islamist actors and the prerequisites of Islamist politics that try to contain them within the limits of collective action and communitarian good. Once again, women's issues are decisive in the unfolding dynamics of these tensions. The forbidden boundaries of the public sphere are drawn by the obstruction of women's visibility. But as women give voice to their aspirations and occupy new professional, political, and urban spaces, they engender a subversive process, albeit independent of their intentions and will.

Islamist women appear at the crossroads of these puzzles because the more they gain public visibility and find a realm of opportunities for their educational and professional ambitions, the more they find themselves in conflict with the traditions or interpretations that prescribe maternal and marital duties as their foremost moral obligations, which forces them to develop new definitions of self. In their own words, they say "no to femininity, yes to personality," thus maintaining their acquiescence to values of modesty, while at the same time opening up an autonomous sphere for their individual aspirations and life-strategies independent of their roles as wives, as mothers, and even as militants of a collective movement.[29] Feminism serves as an intellectual resource in the building of a distinct consciousness of women's identity within the Islamic movement.[30] It has become the source of a line of demarcation between varying interpretations of men and women, but also between women themselves; between those who acquiesce without question to the prescribed traditional gender roles and Islamic militancy and those who develop a criticism of these roles from within, forging new self-definitions. A hybrid Islamic and feminist consciousness initially emerged from below, which was limited to the internal discussions of the movement, leading in the 1990s to more overt expressions in public debate, either through publications (magazines on woman's identity) or through nongovernmental women's organizations.[31]

Every step toward increasing the public visibility of women via Islamist movements triggers a new round of public debate, setting secularists and Islamists in opposition, but also stirring up controversy among the Islamists themselves. For instance, with the end of the state monopoly on broadcasting, commercial broadcasting has rendered Islam visible and ubiquitous on Turkish television.[32] Yet the presence of women, the image of uncovered or covered women on Islamic television channels, continues to be the line of demarcation separating different trajectories of the Islamic public sphere and the ideological positions of Islamism. Similarly, the proliferation of private Islamic radio stations opens up a new realm of job opportunities for Islamic women journalists, but the issue of "women's voice," considered by some a provocation and thus illicit, renders women's professional presence precarious and questions its legitimacy. For some literalist Muslim theologians, women's voice is also considered *awra*,[33] banning women's performance in front of a mixed public.

Another example of these paradoxes of Islamic public visibility can be found in tourism and the changing consumption patterns of the newly formed Islamic middle classes. The popularity of a new luxurious hotel (Caprice Hotel) that offers summer vacations in conformity with Islamic rules—organizing activities in conformity with prayer hours, serving only non-alcoholic beverages, providing separate beaches and swimming pools for men and women, with Islamic swimwear for both sexes—testify well to the degree to which Islamist identity difference is inseparable from consumption, commodity, property, and even pleasure patterns dictated by global and local trends of the market economy. Islamist intellectuals advocating resistance and authenticity criticize such integrative and conformist strategies as an attempt to strengthen the Islamist movement by means of the Western lifestyle of consumption and vacation. Yet for many members of the newly formed middle classes, vacation is as natural as working; neither can be given up merely because they are allegedly Western.

An Autobiographical Novel by a Young Islamist

A novel written by a young Islamist writer is an example of a more self-reflexive mode of changing Muslim subjectivities as an unfolding process of political Islamism. This novel, written by Mehmet Efe, can be considered an autobiographical narrative bearing witness to his own and his generation's Islamism.[34] The title of the novel, *Mızraksız İlmihal*, refers to a very well known religious manual from the sixteenth century that was widely used in both the Ottoman Empire and Turkey among observant Muslims. *İlmihal* is a kind of Islamic catechism, an elementary level religious education pamphlet concerning faith, creed, forms of worship, and morality and focusing on topics such as ablution, prayer, articles of faith, and the five pillars of Islam. *Mızraklı* means "something or someone with spears." The contemporary author plays with the words by adding to it a negative suffix *sız* (without) and turns *mızraklı* into *mızraksız*. This linguistic twist makes the reader think of a catechism without spears and conveys a sense of faith without compulsion.

The writer, in his twenties, tells a story of the Islamist generation during the post-1980 period. His narrative of an Islamist male student of his own age provides us with additional clues and images that can help clarify our definitions of an Islamist and of radical Islamism. Irfan (the word means knowledge, which is described as the pillar of the civilizations of the East) is a student in the history department of Istanbul University. He defines himself as part of the general Islamist movement; that is, he is "Muslim, religious, Islamist, radical revolutionary, fundamentalist, pro-Iranian, Sufi, etc. ..." (78). He is a typical representative of the students in the Islamist movements of the post-1980s, coming from a provincial town, originally from the lower middle class with a traditional religious family background, and becoming an Islamist at the university when he arrives in a large city like Istanbul. His life exhibits upward social mobility, since he is the first of his family to gain access to higher education and urban life. He depicts his student life as the life of a political Islamist and an activist: collective prayers in mosques, followed by political demonstrations against Israel and the United States, participation in panels, and visits to Islamic bookstores are the activities and spaces that he is familiar with. In the corridors of the university and on the streets of Istanbul, he acts as an Islamist revolutionary: "We were actors, heroes of the images in our dreams incited by the Iranian revolution" (16). Acquiring political consciousness empowers him in his relations with girls as well: "Before, when a girl asked me a question, I was so perplexed, not knowing what to do . . . afterwards, that is after acquiring political consciousness . . . finding myself among the people who believe in liberation, salvation through Islam, girls didn't appear to me important enough to be taken seriously . . . and those who were covered [*read Islamist*], were my sisters [*bacım*]. They were the pioneers and mothers of the society that I was dreaming of and struggling for" (15).

This narrative of an Islamist student is almost the exact mirror-image of a revolutionary leftist student in the 1970s in Turkey. Each has a dream of an ideal society, a utopia for liberation and salvation; for each this implies a radical, that is, a complete revolutionary change of the society. In both cases, the life of a revolutionary necessitates giving up the pleasures or necessities of daily life as a male and as a student, pleasures considered trivial compared to the exigencies of the upcoming revolution and bracketed until the arrival of that day. As militants and missionaries, they commit to and project themselves into the future ideal society. In other words, for the sake of public ideals and political revolution, private, intimate identities and relations are given up. Ironically, male actors of leftism and Islamism both empower themselves politically in repressing their male identities and thus reproducing the dominant values of a communitarian morality that tolerates male-female socialization only within the accepted boundaries of sisters, mothers, or comrades.

The young Islamist character of the novel was not able to radically change his society, but he did go through a radical change when he fell in love with an Islamist coed. The girl, as a new image of Muslim woman, and the deep love he develops for her present a constant challenge to his political convictions and collective commitments. Being in love with her triggers a catharsis in his personal change and emerging new Muslim self.

The girl represents those female actors of contemporary Islamism who are self-assertive and yearning for educational success. Boy meets girl on registration day at the university: Islamists are protesting the prohibition of Islamic veiling, and he asks her to participate in the boycott. She retorts with feminist irony and criticism, advancing her individual identity (and her preference for registering). She does not accept that men speak and act on behalf of women: "Did you ask my opinion for the action? You men make speeches, satisfy yourself exhibiting heroic actions, and we should be the decoration, ha?" (17). Furthermore, she mocks the male activists of Islamism: "Protesting became a fixation for you ... You feel an inferiority complex in relation to leftists? Is that why you impatiently jumped on our headscarves?" (32).

The female character, Nurcan, is a typical representative of Islamist female actors of the 1980s and 1990s: self-affirming, educated, urban, and critical. Her role in the novel exemplifies Islamist women as generators of change and not merely acquiescing to the logic of the movement. She is a duplicate of the Islamist women characters changing the movement from within as described in my book *The Forbidden Modern*—but with a significant difference. The novel follows but also exceeds the latent dynamics depicted in *The Forbidden Modern* and renders them manifest from the point of view of a male protagonist of Islamism.

Falling in love with one of the new kind of Islamic girls ("it would have been so much simpler with a traditional, docile girl from a village," he complains) plays a cathartic role in his questioning of revolutionary political Islamism. She is an intellectual pioneer in this criticism. We read in her words, taken from her diary: "Such an absurdity! The majority of us start taking seriously the roles we want to play ... They are walking in the corridors as if they were going to realize the revolution tomorrow.... Some among us even say things such as 'Muslim men are too passive.' Everyone is rapidly on the way to 'masculinization' [*erkeksilesiyor*]" (49). Another quotation from her diary can better explain her predicament and reticence toward male-dominated political Islamism: "They [men] also put some books into my hands. Books with phrases that put on my shoulders the obligation to be a warrior, a guerrilla, to take the responsibility for a war that would change everything and the world fundamentally . . . I am small. I am weak. I am a girl. I am just a girl . . . GIRL!" (50–51). Hence, as she appropriates her identity as a young girl, she resists the political and collective roles ascribed to her. Ironically, her weakness, her withdrawal to the intimate, private life, and the boundaries of identity constitute a new source of power to criticize the Islamic ambitions of radical change.

At the end of his journey for change, Irfan, the male character, echoes her words, writing of his desire to distance himself from political militant Islamism: "I want to take off this militant uniform [*parka*] . . . I want to exist not with my enmities but with my friendships . . . I want to satisfy myself with small things. I cannot carry universal things on my shoulders any longer" (171–73). Rediscovering the private "small" life provides an anchor for him to limit the totalizing nature of the Islamist project. Love reintroduces desire, intimacy, and privacy. Falling in love with a woman is already problematic for an Islamist, because, in the words of Irfan, "a Muslim does not fall in love with a woman, but only with Allah" (19). For the first time, and to his own surprise, he starts to share with his friends a "personal" subject, his love for this woman. At the end of the novel, he starts searching for a job and dreams of their life as a happily married couple, imagining himself buying her a colorful dress and a silk headscarf, sharing daily life, cooking and reading together, and so forth.

To consider this novel, which became quite popular among Islamic youth, as a criticism of Islamism from within, as many

Islamic radicals do, would be an oversimplification. The themes of falling in love and looking for a job can both be considered as evidence that the protagonist gives up his commitment to Islamism. But I would argue that the novel testifies to and contributes to the development from collective political Islamism toward the emergence of Muslim subjectivities. The writer, using a modern tool of self-reflexivity—the novel, a literary genre—gives voice to and subjectivizes the Muslim. To do this, he needs to overcome the repressiveness of the collective definitions of Islamic identity. This is the site of the paradox. On the one hand, political Islamism empowers Muslim actors and identity, but on the other it hinders them from expressing themselves in their subjectivities. The novel takes a step forward in the Islamic movement's story in that the author narrates the emerging Muslim subject, who initially owes his existence to the collective political movement, but who no longer needs confrontational politics for his identity. It can be read as the normalization of Muslim identity. The novel tells us the story of a young Islamist transformed by the relationship of love with a member of the "other" sex. The revolutionary role of love in the construction of the subject is decisive. As Alain Touraine writes, "it is because self-consciousness cannot reveal the subject that the emergence of the subject within an individual is so closely bound up with relations with the other . . . The love relationships do away with social determinisms and give the individual a desire to be an actor, to invent a situation, rather than to conform to one . . . It is thanks to the relationship with the other as subject that individuals cease to be functional elements of the social system and become their own creators and the producers of society."[35] Hence, when our male character criticizes political Islamism and gives up antisystemic resistance, he is not simply conforming to given values of modernity but, on the contrary, is appropriating, blending, and composing between self and modernity.

The genre of the novel, both as an expression of self-reflexivity and exposure of the self in public, is inseparable from the birth of the modern individual. Self-reflexivity and self-exposure in public are not traits of societies where communitarian values of modesty prevail. Hence, as Farzaneh Milani argues, the absence of autobiography as a genre in Persian (but also in Turkish) literature demonstrates the "reluctance to talk publicly and freely about the self," a condition found not only in women, who are "privatized" but also in men, who are expected to be "self-contained."[36]

Mehmet Efe's autobiographical novel testifies to the newly emerging Muslim male-female subjectivities in the public sphere, which in turn constitute a challenge to the Islamist movement.[37] Against the totalizing ideal of Islamism, the novel carves out a space for intimacy and privacy that resists the monitoring of the personal by the public. It thus expresses the "self-limiting radicalism"[38] of Islamism and thereby counters the totalitarian tendencies embedded in Islamist politics. In other terms, the frontiers of the forbidden Islamic public sphere are challenged from within by the intrusion of Muslim male-female intimacies. Love constitutes a resistance to the suppression of male-female subjectivities and the puritanization of the public sphere.

More than twenty years after the publication of this first

autobiographical novel by an Islamist, we observe a proliferation of male and female subjectivities expressed in novels,[39] media, and art. Alternative spaces for Muslim modes of sociability, such as coffee houses,[40] restaurants, and hotels characterize the opening of the public space to religious norms. In the last three decades, Islam has acquired new forms of visibility with Muslim actors making their way in the public avenues of both Muslim and European societies. New faces of Muslim actors using both secular and religious idiom appear in public life; the terms of public debate are transformed by the eruption of religious issues; Islamic films and novels become popular in cultural criticism; new alternative spaces, markets, and media open up in response to rising demands of recently formed Muslim middle classes. Islam carves out a public space of its own as new Islamic language styles, corporeal rituals, and spatial practices emerge and blend into public life. On the one hand, public Islam testifies to a shift in the orientation of the Islamic movement from macropolitics toward everyday life micropractices. On the other hand, it challenges the national borders and the secular principles of the public sphere.

6 Public Islam

New Visibilities and New Imaginaries

n this chapter, I will discuss the visual aspect of the divide between the religious and the secular by tracing the ways in which Muslim actors enter into secular public spaces. Islam has acquired new forms of visibility in the last two decades, as it makes its way in the public avenues of both Muslim and European societies. New faces of Muslim actors using both secular and religious idiom appear in public life. The terms of public debates are transformed by the eruption of religious issues. Islamic films and novels become popular in cultural criticism, and new spaces, markets, and media open up in response to rising demands of recently formed Muslim middle classes. Islam carves out a public space of its own as new Islamic language styles, corporeal rituals, and spatial practices emerge and blend into public life. On the one hand, public Islam testifies to a shift in the orientation of the Islamic movement from macropolitics toward micropractices, and on the other, it challenges the borders and the meanings of the secular public sphere.

As Islam makes a move into national public spheres, the consensual principles and homogeneous structure of the national public spheres are unsettled, but so are those of the Islamic movement. Indeed two different phases of contemporary Islamism can be distinguished.[1] The first phase, starting at the end of the 1970s and reaching its peak with the Iranian Islamic revolution in 1979, is characterized by mass mobilizations, Islamic militancy, a quest for an Islamic collective identity, and the implementation of a political and religious rule. In the second phase, the revolutionary fervor declines, the ideological chorus gives way to a multiplicity of voices, and a process of distancing and individuation from the collective militancy takes place, leading to an "exit from religious revolution."[2] In this phase, after the assertion of a collective and exacerbated form of difference, Muslim identity is in the process of normalization. In the second phase of Islamism, actors of Islam blend into modern urban spaces, use global communication networks, engage in public debates, follow consumption patterns, learn market rules, enter into secular time, get acquainted with values of individuation, professionalism, and consumerism, and reflect on their new practices. Hence we observe a transformation of these movements from a radical political stance to a more social and cultural orientation, accompanied by a loss of mass mobilization capacity, which led some researchers to pronounce the end of Islamism and the failure of political Islam.[3] However, a more cultural orientation does not mean a less political one. Indeed, instead of disappearing as a reference, Islam penetrates even more into the social fabrics and imaginaries, thereby raising new political questions, questions not addressed solely to Muslims but concerning the foundational principles of collective life in general.

An analytical concern at the level of ideologies (such as Islamism) or of political formations (such as the state) cannot explain this process of interpenetration and dialogical relation. The public visibility of Islam and the specific gender, corporeal, and spatial practices underpinning it trigger new ways of imagining a collective self and common space that are distinct from the Western liberal self and progressive politics. Exploring these Islamic makings of the self and the micropractices associated with it will lead us to understand new social imaginaries and the transformations of the public sphere in a non-Western context.

Non-Western Publics

Although the idea of the public is Western in its origins and its basic features are understood as universal access, individualism, equality, and openness (*offentlichkeit*), it circulates and moves into contexts other than the West. The ways in which these concepts, ideas, and institutions travel and are adopted in non-Western contexts depend on local agencies and cultural fields. The experience of colonization in India, for instance, or voluntary modernization in Turkey, has shaped the ways in which the public sphere is imagined and institutionalized. Studying the adoption of modern concepts at the level of language, their entry, translations, and transformations—namely the historical semantics (*Begriffsgechichte*)—can reveal the diversity of meanings and trajectories and hint at the particular conjunctions between the universal definitions of the public sphere and home-grown practices and idioms.[4] The articulations and tensions between two different cultural codes, modern and indigenous, intervene in distinguishing and defining public and private spheres, interior and exterior spaces, definition and meanings of licit and illicit practices. Sometimes they are simply juxtaposed in mutual indifference, sometimes they compete with each other, and sometimes they engage in a dialogue that produces interpenetrations and displacements. Conception of the exterior space, civility in the European sense of order and discipline, can therefore take on different meanings and forms in non-Western contexts. To indicate the differences

between a Brahminical concept of cleanliness and purity and a Western concept of hygiene, Sudipta Kaviraj describes how the exteriors of houses in India are abandoned to an intrinsic disorderliness, while the interiors are kept impressively clean.[5] The interior, intimate, gendered space is similarly valorized and highly disciplined in Muslim societies, leading to different conceptualizations and institutionalizations of the modern public and city life. Although the cultural program of modernity has a great capacity to influence and circulate, the encounter between the two cultural codes leads not to a simple logic of emulation or rejection but to improvisations in social practices and cultural meanings. Studying the public sphere as a social imaginary may offer new clues to map out these improvisations in a non-Western context.

The social imaginary is, as Cornelius Castoriadis tells us, "the creation of significations and the creation of the images and figures that support these significations."[6] There is an "essential historicity of significations: apparently similar 'institutions' can be radically other, since immersed in another society, they are caught up in other significations."[7] Institutions are not to be conceived as external to social imaginaries and social practices. There is no institution without signification, but the signification is not legitimate without shared practices. Although the "original" European code of modernity has constituted the crucial starting point and continual reference point, it is continuously and creatively appropriated and altered. Therefore, these distinct cultural foundations and institutional formations should be analyzed, as Shmuel N. Eisenstadt and Wolfgang Schluchter remind us, "not only in terms of their approximation to the West but also in their own terms."[8] An analysis of the public sphere as a social imaginary can illustrate the circulation of a universal code of modernity as well as the particular significations and practices. Approaching the public sphere as a social imaginary in Castoriadis's sense emphasizes its dynamic aspect, as an ongoing process, a creation of significations and practices rather than an "imagined" and "pre-established" frame. Furthermore it defies the thesis of time-lag and "deficiency of modernity"[9] for non-Western countries and gives intellectual credibility to societal practices in historical contexts other than the West; it suggests the possibility for *Imaginary Institution of Society*.

The public sphere in a non-Western context is neither identical with its counterparts in the West, nor entirely dissimilar, but manifests asymmetrical differences as it is continuously altered by a field of cultural meanings and social practices. Modern social imaginaries, as Charles Taylor reminds us, are social in the sense that they are widely and commonly shared.[10] They may have explicit theoretical formulations, but unlike ideas and ideologies they are not in the hands of a few. Social imaginaries are embedded in the habitus of a population, or carried in implicit understandings that underlie and make possible common practices. Even in cases where the public sphere is introduced by colonizing agents or adopted by modernizing elites, it cannot be understood as an alien structure or as an imposed idea from above. As a social imaginary, the public sphere works in a social field and penetrates and blends into cultural significations.

In the Turkish context of voluntary modernization, the public sphere is institutionalized and imagined as a site for the implementation of a secular and progressive way of life. An authoritarian modernism—rather than bourgeois, individualist liberalism—underpins this public sphere. Religious signs and practices have been silenced as the modern public sphere has set itself against the Muslim social imaginary and segregated social organization; modern codes of conduct have entered public spaces ranging from the Parliament and educational institutions to the street and public transportation. In a Muslim context, women's participation in public life, corporeal visibility, and social mixing with men all count as modern. The modern gendered subject has been constituted through female role models and repetitive performances, including language styles, dress codes, modes of habitation, and modes of address.

Here we see the social imaginary of the public sphere at work. While it adheres to some of the basic universal principles of the Western public sphere, these principles are selectively highlighted, coupled, and translated into social practices that are creatively altered as well. The central stakes of the modern subject are worked out in tension with Muslim definitions of self; consequently the access of women to public life and gender equality acquires a more relevant signification in the public imaginary of Muslim societies. Moreover, in non-Western contexts, the public sphere provides a stage for the didactic performance of the modern subject in which the nonverbal, corporeal, and implicit aspects of social imaginaries are consciously and explicitly worked out. Because the public sphere provides a stage for performance rather than an abstract frame for textual and discursive practices, the ocular aspect in the creation of significations and the making of social imaginaries becomes of utmost importance. Social imaginaries are carried by images. The body, as a sensorial and emotional register, links the implicit nonverbal practices and learned dispositions (namely habitus) into a public visibility and conscious meaning. Public visibility refers to the techniques of working from the inside out, transforming implicit practices into observable and audible ones. This chapter explores the centrality of gender as well as related corporeal regimens and spatial protocols in the making of the public sphere.

The ways in which Islam emerges in the public sphere defy modernist aspirations for a civilized (read Westernized) and emancipated self, yet follow a similar pattern in regard to gender, body, and space issues. The covered woman deputy walking into the Turkish Parliament and walking out the same day serves as an icon: an image that crystallizes the tensions emanating from two different cultural programs in the making of the self and the public—a visibility that by the same token reveals the ways in which Parliament as a secular public sphere is imagined, constructed, and instituted in the Turkish republican context. Therefore a two-layered reading is required. One concerns the modern self-presentation and its migration into the Turkish context of modernity. The second concerns the counterattack of Islamic practices as a competing form of pious self-making and social imaginary. And with this second reading, through an examination of the ways in which Islam is problematized in the public sphere, we become aware of the unspoken, implicit borders and the stigmatizing, exclusionary power structure of the secular public sphere.

The Headscarf in the Turkish Parliament: A "Blow-up"

For the first time in its republican history, Turkey witnessed the election of a covered Muslim woman, an Istanbul deputy from the pro-Islamic Fazilet Partisi (Virtue Party) during the general elections in 1999. But it was Merve Kavakçı's physical presentation in the Parliament, not her election, that provoked a public dispute, a blow-up. On the very day of its opening on May 2, 1999, Kavakçı, a thirty-one-year-old woman, wearing a white headscarf with fashionable frameless eyeglasses and a long-skirted, modern two-piece suit walked (over)confidently into the meeting hall of the National Assembly for the opening session of the new Parliament. The men and women deputies stood up and protested against Kavakçı's presence with such vehemence that she was obliged to leave the Parliament without taking the oath.[11] This forced exit was accompanied by shouting like: "Merve out, ayatollahs to Iran!" and "Turkey is secular, will remain secular!" Kavakçı's Islamic covering challenged the unwritten laws of the Parliament and enraged the deputies as well as (secular) public opinion.[12] The most well known secular women's association organized meetings and condemned the headscarf in the Parliament as an "ideological uniform of Islamic fundamentalism," which threatens republican state power and hard-earned secular rights and liberties made possible by Kemalist reforms.[13] Kavakçı was treated as an agent provocateur in the Turkish press, which accused her of having close links with the Palestinian group Hamas and working for foreign powers such as Iran and Libya. It was discovered that Kavakçı had become a U.S. citizen shortly after becoming a parliamentary candidate. As she had not officially declared that she was holding another passport, authorities were able to use this legal pretext to strip Kavakçı of her Turkish citizenship.[14]

The above story cannot be narrated as merely a political incident. At a microlevel, instantaneous social reality and the significant tensions that generate history can be condensed and concealed. The trivial can be revealed as meaningful. In Georg Simmel's words, in these "momentary images," snapshots (*Momentbilder*), fragments of social reality, we are able to glimpse the meaning of the whole.[15] We can unpack the nature of the social discord between the secular and religious practices compressed in this political incident if we first take it as it is, that is, frame it as a picture or snapshot. Visualizing the story and the players will bring into focus the corporeal, gendered, and spatial aspects of the social cleavages. Second, we need to defamiliarize our gaze. The picture is taken from the present day. It is widely and commonly shared. Its accessibility makes its understanding even more difficult, because it appears as ordinary and natural to the common eye, duplicating the given terms of public controversy. This trompe l'oeil poses a challenge to sociology. A sign must be interpreted using "thick description" and placed in historical perspective, if we want to reveal all of its possible meanings.[16] We need to go back and forth between micro- and macrolevels of analysis, between empirical practices and theoretical readings.[17] If we introduce anthropological unfamiliarity, historical distance, and the shift between micro- and macrolevels, the ordinary will appear less ordinary, and the still picture will turn into a movie. In his film *Blow-up* (1966), Michelangelo Antonioni tells the story of a photographer who by chance takes a picture that appears at first incoherent and incomprehensible. But then he enlarges a detail of the photograph, and that one detail leads him to read the whole picture differently.[18] Let's enlarge—blow up—the picture of the veiled deputy taken in the public sphere.

Merve Kavakçı's portrait is both representative and distinctive in relation to other Muslim women in the Islamic movement. The trajectory of this Muslim woman deputy follows a social dynamic similar to that of Islamic female students who have sought the right to attend university classes wearing headscarves since the beginning of the 1980s.[19] Access to higher education, daily experience of urban city life, and use of political idiom and action expose new female Islamic actors to modernity; this exposure is problematic for both secular actors and religious ones. The case of Merve Kavakçı, though not an exception, serves as an example that carries the process of interaction with a program of modernity to its extreme limits; it thereby blurs the oppositional boundaries. Kavakçı had access to higher education, became a computer engineer, trained at the University of Texas (because the headscarf was then banned in Turkish universities), lived in the United States, had two children, divorced her Jordanian-American husband, returned to Turkey, and became a member of the pro-Islamic party. She had access therefore to powerful symbols of modernity and was simultaneously engaged in Islamic politics. Living in the United States (not in Saudi Arabia), speaking English fluently, using new technologies, fashioning a public image (light-colored headscarf and frameless eye-glasses) are all cultural symbols of distinction in a non-Western context of modernity. And Islamists are not insensitive to acquiring such cultural capital. In fact, though they are in an oppositional political struggle with the modern secularists, they often mirror them and search for public representatives who speak foreign languages and belong to the professional and intellectual elite. Even Kavakçı's choice of a two-piece suit rather than an overcoat is a duplication of the republican women's dress code. With all of her elite credentials, Kavakçı could have been used to bolster Islamic pride—if only she was not so "foreign."[20]

Her trajectory is not only a sign of distinction; it also distinguishes her from other Muslim women and brings her socially closer to the Western-oriented, secular elites of Turkey. It is a closeness that creates more enmity than sympathy. The appropriation of social signs of modernity, such as language, comportment, politics, public exposure, and being in contact with secular groups, without giving up the Islamic difference (marked by the headscarf), is the source of trouble. It is the "small difference" and the small distance between her and the secular women that ignite political passion. Only when there is this feeling of a stranger's intrusion into one's own domain, places, and privileges is there an issue of rejection or recognition of difference. The figure of the stranger, in a Simmelian approach, represents the ambivalent relation of proximity and distance, identity and difference, through which a group reproduces social life and hierarchically structures social space.[21] This is why the small difference is so crucial in understanding the rejection of those that are closest.

In Turkey, one of the arguments widely used against the headscarf was that it had been appropriated as a political symbol, so the desire to wear it was not a disinterested one. Many would say they were not against their grandmother's headscarf; on the contrary, they remembered it with affection and respect. This is certainly true to the extent that grandmothers either sat in their corners at home and didn't step into the sites of modernity or took off their headscarves as they walked out from indoors. Such behavior was in conformity with the scenario of national progress and emancipation of women, key elements of the modern social imaginary in a non-Western context. But now the play as well as the actors has changed. The Islamic headscarf is deliberately appropriated, not passively carried and handed down from generation to generation. It is claimed by a new generation of women who have had access to higher education, notwithstanding their modest social origins (many come from the periphery of the big cities or from small towns). Instead of assimilating to the secular regime of women's emancipation, they press for their embodied difference (e.g., Islamic dress) and their public visibility (e.g., in schools, in Parliament), and create disturbances in modern social imaginaries. Islamic women hurt the feelings of secular women and upset the status quo; they are playing with ambivalence, being both Muslim and modern without wanting to give up one for the other. They are outside a regime of imitation: critical of both subservient traditions and assimilative modernity. One can almost twist the argument and say that they are neither Muslim nor modern. The ambiguity of signs disturbs both the traditional Muslim and the secular modernist social groups. And this goes further than a question of abstract identity. It takes place in the public sphere, it involves a face-to-face relation, which means that difference is marked on the body; it is an embodied difference, one that is visible to others. Islamic visibility (and not solely the identity) creates such a malaise because it has a corporeal, ocular, and spatial dimension. These dimensions are only intensified in the case of Merve Kavakçı.

She was both a local and a "foreigner" (in a literal sense as well, given that she became a U.S. citizen); she was from here, but also from elsewhere. Her popular background and her choice for a headscarf recalled the indigenous yet "pre-modern" Turkey, while her education, individualistic posture, and political language belonged to the modern world; she was a woman who followed an Islamic dress code yet did not adopt the traditional dress, behavior, and representations. Professional and political ambitions, as well as divorce, are all indicators of a nontraditional life and personality. Furthermore, that she did not collapse into tears under heavy pressure and criticism, and does not speak the collective language of those who were persecuted, interposes a psychological distance between her and the Muslim community. The latter uses widely the idiom of suffering and victimization and through common emotional practices, such as crying and lamenting, reproduces a repertoire of cultural signs, a sense of social belonging, and a collective social movement. Meanwhile Kavakçı's individualist and composed self-presentation created trouble in the Islamic social imaginary. Secular women, too, were no less suspicious of her "cold-blooded attitude"; it was taken as one more strike against her, revealing her militant discipline and premeditated behavior at the service of a political conspiracy. Kavakçı cannot be situated in terms of geographical location, communitarian belonging, or cultural coding; as she crossed the boundaries and circulated among different locations—thereby placing them in disjunctive relation to one another—new social imaginaries were being shaped.[22]

Kavakçı's fearlessness in the face of intimidation and her insensitivity to established relations of domination between Muslim and secularist women were perceived as arrogant, but at the same time her carriage and discourse changed the codes of interaction. Her political language was that of constitutional rights, which resonated more in a United States–style democracy than in Turkey, where the constitution tended to provide more trouble than rights. Her language made reference to an ultramodern space, whereas her covered body suggested Muslim privacy and modesty. She was from "here" but also from "elsewhere"; but she was neither a replica of a local Muslim actor, nor a Western other. On the one hand, she was not less modern than the Turkish women defending the secular national public sphere. On the other hand, her persistent wearing of the Islamic headscarf displayed her embodied difference and reproduced and deepened the cleavage. The ambiguous signs carried by her presence created confusion and disturbance among Muslims but also among secularists (including the journalists from CNN to whom her American-inflected language was more familiar). The fact that she came from "elsewhere" and made reference to another mental space disturbed—and also helped to transgress—the social rules of conduct and interaction. As Goffman writes, the rupture of the framework is used by those from below, trying to discredit and disturb an adversary.[23] Such surprising crossovers bring into question the fixity of categories and boundaries.

The social dispute generated by the public visibility of Islam is carried by corporeal performances and self-presentations rather than by textualized forms of subjectivities and discursive practices. The public sphere is not simply a preestablished arena; it is constituted and negotiated through performance. In addition to constituting the public sphere, these micropractices enact a way of being public. We can speak of what Victor Turner calls "performative reflexivity." It is a "condition in which a sociocultural group, or its most perceptive members acting representatively, turn, bend, or reflect back upon themselves, upon the relations, actions, symbols, meanings, and codes, roles, statuses, social structures, ethical and legal rules, and other sociocultural components which make up their public 'selves.'"[24] Islamic performance has a reflexive character to the extent that the codes and symbols embedded in the religious culture are critically appropriated and distanced from the traditional culture. The Islamic dress code exemplifies this performative reflexivity. The practice of veiling restores a link with past traditions; it signifies the immutability of religion and nonsecular time. Through repetition, rehearsal, and performance, the practice of veiling is reproduced again and again, acquiring legitimacy and authority and contributing to the making of modest pious self. But the veiling is not derived directly from prevailing cultural habits and preestablished conventions. On the contrary, it bears a new form, the outcome of a selective and reflexive attitude that amplifies and dramatizes the performative signs of difference. It is transgressive with respect to Muslim traditions as well as to modern self-presentations. Consequently, the new covering suggests a more rather than less potent Islam, which accounts for secular counterattacks against the headscarf for being not an innocent religious convention, but a powerful political symbol. Let's turn our gaze back to secularist counterattacks. A brief detour to the linkage between women and the making of the public sphere will introduce a historical perspective into the picture without which we cannot explain the destabilizing force of Islam in secular social imaginaries. One has to remember that Turkish secularist women have entered into modernity through emancipation from religion, which was symbolized by taking off the veil. They have experimented with modernity as a tangible entity inscribed on their bodies, clothes, and ways of life—and not exclusively as an abstract and distant category of citizenship. They are products of a historical, emotional, corporeal fracture with the Muslim identity, a fracture with the past that made it possible for them to have access to modernity.

The grand narratives on modernity typically describe the elements of modernity in non-Western contexts as insufficient. However, when the concepts of Western modernity travel into different contexts, they often acquire not only different meanings but also an unexpected intensity. Secularism is an example of this phenomenon. Secularism, because of its origins in the Western historical development, is expected to be a marginal element in other contexts, especially in Muslim ones. Yet in the Turkish case, for instance, we observe not only its role in nation-state building and its penetration into civil and military elite ideology, but also its emergence in civil society and in particular in women's associations. Secularism works as a social imaginary.

151

It is possible to speak of an excess of secularism, when secularism becomes a fetish of modernity. Modern social imaginaries cross boundaries and circulate but take a different twist and a slightly modified accent in non-Western contexts—they take on a sense of *extra*. We can read extra both as external to the West and as additional and unordinary. The evolutionary concept of historical change can hardly imagine that there can be a surplus or excess of modernity in some domains of social life in non-Western contexts. Modernity functions as a fetish. In non-Western contexts, modernity's manifestations are overemphasized, as are the performances of belonging to modernity.[25] The excess of secularism in Muslim contexts of modernity is such an example. The public sphere becomes a site for modern and secular performances. In contrast with the formation of the public sphere in the West, characterized initially as a bourgeois sphere that excluded the working classes and women, in Muslim contexts of modernity, women function as a pivotal sign/site in the making and representing of the public sphere.[26]

As discussed in the previous chapter, in a Muslim context, women's visibility and the social mixing of men and women attest to the existence of a public sphere. Women as public citizens and women's rights are more relevant than citizenship and civil rights in the Turkish modern imaginary. Women's participation in public life as citizens and as civil servants, their visibility in urban spaces, and their socialization with men all define the modern secular way of life and indicate a radical shift from the social organization and gender roles framed by Islam. In other words, in a Muslim context, secularism denotes a modern way of life, calling for the emancipation of women from religion, the removal of the veil, and the end of the gender-segregated spatial organizations. Women are symbols of the social whole: home and outside, interior and exterior, private and public. They stand in for the making of the modern individual, for the modern ways of being private and public. Women's corporeal and civic visibility as well as the formation of heterosocial spaces underpins the stakes of modernity in a Muslim society.

Secularism is enacted as a modern social imaginary through gendered, corporeal, and spatial performances. In that respect, some common spaces are transformed as they gain additional symbolic value and become public sites of visual modernity and gendered secular performances. In addition to Parliament, schools, and the workplace, spaces such as beaches, opera and concert halls, coffeehouses, fashion shows, public gardens, and public transportation all become sites for modern self-presentations. They are instituted and imagined as public spaces through these daily micropractices in which men and women rehearse and improvise in public their new self-presentations, dress codes, bodily postures, aesthetic and cultural tastes, and leisure activities.

The implicit dimensions of modern social imaginaries, namely the aspects that are embodied in the habitus of a population, in the modes of address, living, habitation, and taste, all become explicit features of performative modernity in a non-Western context. The public sphere denotes a space for the making of the new modern self, while it excludes others, namely those who do not conform to this new life and new habitus—observant Muslims, for example. Acts of performance as well as space are not socially neutral concepts; indeed they are situated in and produced by social relations of domination and exclusion.

As Henri Lefevbre puts it, the notion of space refers not to an empty space but to a space of production of social relations, defining boundaries of exclusion and inclusion, of the licit and illicit.[27] Social space, moreover, implies virtual or actual assembling at a point; urban space brings together the masses, products, markets, acts, and symbols. It concentrates them, accumulates them. Speaking about urban space invokes as well a center and a centrality, actual or possible.[28] Through its invocation of the possibility of assembly and commonality, public space establishes its link with democracy.

The issue of recognition arises when the Other, perceived as different, becomes closer in proximity—spatially, socially, and corporeally. Recognition of difference is possible only when one finds similitude and commonality with the other. One has to discern the "concrete Other"—single individuals with life histories—in order to be able to tolerate difference as part of a social bond.[29] Over-politicized definitions of identity and arguments of conspiracy exclude the possibility of finding semblance and familiarity; indeed, they reinforce the demoniacal definitions of the adversary. In Merve Kavakçı's case, she was not recognized as a woman, an individual, a Muslim, a deputy, and a citizen, but rejected and stigmatized as a militant, an Islamist, and an outsider.

The question of a social bond with the stigmatized and excluded Other is the essential problem of democracy.[30] In the case of Islam in the public sphere, there is a double movement that causes uneasiness: Islamists seek to enter into spaces of modernity, yet they display their distinctiveness. There is a problem of recognition to the extent that Islamists start sharing the same spaces of modernity, such as the Parliament, university classes, television programs, beaches, opera halls, and coffeehouses, and yet they fashion a counter-Islamic self. In contrast with being a Muslim, being an Islamist entails a reflexive performance; it involves collectively constructing, assembling, and restaging the symbolic materials to signify difference. The symbols of Muslim habitus are reworked, selectively processed, and staged in public. Performative acts of religious difference in the secular public space defy the limits of recognition and of social bonds, unsettling thereby modern social imaginaries.

The Islamic critique of modernity can be interpreted as a new stage in the process of the indigenization of modernity in non-Western contexts. The Islamic subject is formed both through liberation from traditional definitions and roles of Muslim identity and through resistance to a cultural program of modernity and liberalism. Alain Touraine claims that the subject owes her existence to a social conflict or collective action that criticizes the established order, expected roles, and logic of power.[31] Thus the Islamic subject is created by a collective action that is critical of the subjugation of Muslim identity both by community (religious and otherwise) and modernity. The search for difference and authenticity expresses a critical resistance to the assimilative strategies and homogenizing practices of modernity. Especially in non-Western contexts, the reflexive nature of modernity, the critical capacity to surpass its limits, is weak.[32] Criticism of modernity is engendered when modernity becomes an indigenous, everyday practice.

Indigenously defined modernity is not only thought of as a discursive regime that shapes subjectivity but also constituted and negotiated through performances.[33] The Habermasian model of bourgeois public sphere as worked out by "rational-critical debate" does not always provide a frame to understand the performative basis of the indigenously defined modernity. In distinction from the Enlightenment notion of the public sphere, which endorsed gender blindness, gender movements and other identity-based movements display and make public sexual differences.[34] Grasping the meaning of performance of difference through corporeal and spatial practices requires a new reading of nonverbal communication, embodied information, and sensorial interaction.

The nonverbal "embodied information" with its link to "naked senses" provides one of the crucial communication conditions, according to Erving Goffman.[35] And of the sensory organs, the eye has a uniquely sociological function: the union and interaction of individuals are based upon mutual glances.[36] Especially where issues of religion and gender are in question, the vocabulary of gaze and spatial conventions acquire a greater relevance. When Muslim women cross the borders between inside and outside, multiple senses—sight, smell, touch, and hearing—feature in concerns over redefining borders, preserving decency, and separating genders. A public Islam needs to redefine and re-create the borders of the interior, intimate, illicit gendered space (mahrem).[37] The notion of modesty (edep) underpins the Muslim self and her relation to private and public spaces. The veiling suggests the importance of the ocular (avoiding the masculine gaze, casting down one's eyes), and the segregation of spaces regulates gender sociability. These acts, these counteraesthetics, body postures, and modes of address are public performances; they seek to gain authority and legitimacy through their repetitions and rehearsals. They are not alien to Muslim memory and culture. They are rooted in the past traditions and memory, in the religious habitus. But they are not simple conventions that have always been there and that are unconsciously handed down from generation to generation. The habitus provides, in Pierre Bourdieu's account, a source of improvisations; it allows for a process of continual correction and adjustment.[38] However, Islamic public visibilities are not implicitly embodied in Muslim habitus. They mark a break with tradition. Islamism is a political means for the exacerbation of Muslim difference. This process of exacerbation makes the habitus (both secular and religious) explicit and conscious. Grandmother's veiling is acceptable because it is natural, whereas the new veiling is not so innocent because it is not a movement among religious or interior women. Secularists are not wrong to read it as a symbol. Although not rendered discursively, a nonverbal embodied communication in the veil conveys information; it disobeys both traditional and secular ways of imagining self-emancipation and becoming public.

Islamic public visibility presents a critique of a secular version of the public sphere. The work of Richard Sennett has shown that the initial development of the public sphere in the West was inseparable from the ways in which people were experiencing their bodies; the body was linked to urban space by religious rituals.[39] According to Sennett, the dematerialization of the public sphere and its separation from the body is the secular version of the public sphere. The divorce of urban experience from religious understanding inhibits the creation of intense civic bonds and "civic compassion" in a multicultural city.[40] Drawing upon this analysis, one can suggest that Islamic public display recuperates a phenomenon that has been repressed by secularism. This public display attempts to reconstruct the social link between subjectivity and public space through the reintroduction of religious self-fashionings, performances, and rituals. Women are the principal actors in this process as they display the boundaries between private and public, licit and illicit, body and imaginary. Islamism reinforces the boundaries in social relations through regulating bodily practices in public spaces; this regulation, in turn, serves as a public display of

Islamic subjectivity. The Muslim body becomes, for actors of Islamism as well as for secularists, a site for resistance to secular modernity. It is a site where both difference and prohibition are linked to the formation of a new subject (neither Muslim nor modern or both Muslim and modern) and a new sociability. On the one hand, this new subject becomes modern, on the other hand, she incorporates the limits, boundaries, and interdictions; hence it is a "forbidden modern." Self-limitation and self-disciplining go together with becoming modern. Ambivalence, which is a feeling that is normally alien to both the religious and the modern, undergirds the contemporary Muslim psyche. In *Another Modernity, a Different Rationality*, Scott Lash draws on Kant's notion of "reflective judgment" to define ambivalence as a third space, the margin between the same and the other, where difference is more primordial than either in presence or absence, and instead exists as an aporetic space of ambivalence and undecidability.[41]

Castoriadis insists on the complementary nature of social representations—without this complementarity, he writes, society would not be possible. For example, the relation between serf and lord—and feudal society itself—is made possible through the institutions and representations that bind them.[42] However, Islamic social imaginaries and practices are worked out through ambivalence rather than complementarity. Surprising crossovers between Islam and modernity and between secular and religious practices take place, unsettling the fixity of positions and oppositional categories. Turkish experience provides us with a privileged terrain for observing this choreography of ambivalence. Voluntary modernization means a processed and displaced form of Western modernity as well as the absence of a colonial Other against which to direct Islamic oppositional discourse. Mutually inclusive categories create not binary oppositions, counterdiscourses, or emulations, but multifaceted, intertwining, modern performances. This ambivalence operates basically through crossing over, losing one's positionality, and circulating in different spaces, categories, and mental mappings. Rather than resulting in peaceful juxtapositions, hybridities, and augmentations, it is worked out in double negations (neither Muslim nor modern) or double assertions (mahrem/forbidden and modern), ambiguities resulting in fragmented subjectivities and transcultural performances. New social imaginaries are shaped by these circulatory, transcultural, and crossover performances. They are imagined, abstract, and implicit categories; they are carried in images, produced by bodily practices and in physical spaces. Islam displays a new "stage" in the making of modern social imaginaries; a stage in which ocular, corporeal, and spatial aspects underlie social action, confrontation, and cohabitation. It is the intrusion of senses, prelinguistic aspects of communication embodied in habitus, that makes the conflict between secularists and Islam so charged with corporeal stigma, affectivity, and political passion.

As I will discuss in chapter 7, the visual domain is increasingly becoming central in shaping the confrontation between the religious and the secular in European countries. The public controversies over Islam in Europe are taking place in the domain of visual art, revealing the conflicts between the sacred and the secular norms of freedom of expression.

7 Public Culture, Art, and Islam

Turkish-Delight in Vienna

A new European public culture is emerging as a result of the encounter with issues concerning Islam. This is an ongoing process through which Islam, from being an external reference, is becoming an internal one in shaping European self-awareness and politics. The categories of Europe and Islam are inadequate to describe this process; they refer to large, macroscale realities, both too obvious and too vague, to a universal religion (Islam), and a historical entity (Europe). It is difficult to relate them; they convey a sense of separation and fixity whereas the frontiers between the two have become porous at the level of everyday practices and politics. What is at stake is the indigenization of Islam and its reterritorialization in Europe, which calls for a two-way awareness and confrontation; Muslims relate religious beliefs with their secular life experiences in Europe, and in turn Europeans engage with Muslim assertions of religious and cultural difference. The European public culture is potentially being conveyed in these encounters, mirroring practices, and cross-reflexivity. The realm of art emerges in this process as a privileged interface in articulating as well as confronting different publics and cultures.

The incompatibility of these cultural and religious codes and the fact that they cross paths in European public life engenders new forms of confrontation; the domain of visual arts becomes one of the battlegrounds of intercultural (and intercivilizational) conflict as well as that of borrowings and mixings. By European public culture, therefore, I refer to new forms (including aesthetic forms) of intercultural interaction, to a process of mutual interpenetration, in which sexuality, religion, and violence are intertwined in particular ways and play a central role.

To depict the ways in which a European public culture is emerging in its encounter with Islamic difference, I shall first adopt a broad perspective and then narrow it down to a controversy over a statue that was exhibited in the park of a public museum in Vienna in 2007. The statue, titled *Turkish-Delight* and created by the German sculptor Olaf Metzel, represents a headscarf-wearing naked woman. I shall use this example to try to highlight the ways in which the realm of art reveals and fashions the public controversies in relation to Muslim migrants in present-day Europe. Women are central to these controversies as markers of the distinction between private and public, between religious morals and secular liberties, and also between different notions of self and civilization.

Thinking across Civilizations

Before focusing on present-day Europe, let me start by adopting a broad perspective in time and in space to open up our ways of thinking about the relations between different civilizations. *What Time Is It There? The Americas and Islam at the Dawn of*

Modern Times is the title of a book published by Serge Gruzinski, in which he reminds us that Ottomans did not wait until the twenty-first century to be interested in the West, in what was then called the New World, the Americas. A book well known to historians had already been published in 1580 in Istanbul under the title of *The History of Western India* (in Turkish: *Tarih-i Hindi-i Garbi*) that illustrated the interest that Ottomans had in understanding the New World, the Americas, which were referred to as Western India.[1] Likewise, as the author argues, peoples in the New World were interested in the Ottomans. A book published in Mexico in 1606 devoted two chapters to Ottoman history. By juxtaposing two quasi-contemporary texts, namely a chronicle of the New World written in Istanbul and a Directory of Time published in Mexico that focuses extensively on the empire of the Turks, the author brings out the interconnections between two visions, between different civilizations separated in time and in space, that of Islam and of America, irreducibly different yet already, before modern times, aware of each other.[2]

Comparing the incomparable, here Istanbul and Mexico, enables us to open up a new perspective in our readings across civilizations and move away from Euro-centered representations of modernity, which subordinate and obliterate experiences in other parts of the world. Gruzinski's way of thinking across civilizations in the premodern era resonates, in a reverse manner, with that of Huntington's thesis of the "clash of civilizations" in the modern world. What might capture one's attention is that Turkey and Mexico appear central in both accounts, albeit to tell a very different story. In the view of Huntington the two countries do not invalidate his thesis because Turkey and

Mexico are seeking to affiliate with a civilization that is different from their own, and therefore are "torn-between" countries, living the clash within.[3]

Whether the two countries represent "torn between" or "in-between" cultures depends, on the one hand, on our ways of reading social reality, and on the ways history will unfold, on the other. As we can observe in present-day politics, the history of Westernization in Turkey (synonymous with Europeanization for the nineteenth-century reformists) in no way convinced Turkish society to give up its Islamic cultural customs and heritage. Nor did it convince Europeans to embrace Turkey into the European Union. On the contrary, Turkish membership seems less legitimate today in the eyes of many European citizens than in the past, in spite of Turkey's political determination to implement the institutional and judicial reforms that are required by the European Union. The eventual Turkish presence in Europe has created resentment in cultural terms; it is feared that the acceptance of Turkey will undermine European identity and blur European frontiers. Likewise, the Mexican immigrants, who are, according to Huntington, reluctant to participate in the American language, civic rites, and virtues common to all, create a potential threat to the cultural and political integrity of the United States.[4]

Drawing on the examples of Mexico and Turkey, we can argue that both countries, in different ways, have today become markers of frontiers, both geographical and cultural, in relation to the "two Wests": America and Europe. It becomes a question of identity for the West. They ask, "Who are we?" in the mirror reflection of the respective Hispanic and Muslim

164

presence and attempt to distinguish the cultural features specific to American and European culture. One should recall that during the nineteenth and twentieth centuries, the notion of Western civilization was synonymous with the idea of a universal claim to embrace different cultures, nations, and religions of the world. This assertion had a particular impact on non-Western histories. Colonization was carried out in the name of universal modernity as well as voluntary modernization. Turkey and Mexico in this respect are two examples where French positivism and *laïcité*, or secularism, have had an important impact on the minds of national reformists in the respective countries; for them the path of modernization would lead to membership in the civilized nations. The notion of civilization was equated with the prefix Western and modernity was thought to be religion-free. In present-day politics the use of the notion of civilization is undergoing a semantic shift; after being discarded during a period characterized by critiques of Western colonialism, to be followed by that of postmodern cultural relativism, it is coming back again into the public discourse of European countries.[5] But this time instead of assuming universalist garb, the notion of civilization tries to capture the cultural distinctiveness of the European experience, thereafter called European cultural values, in contrast to those of Islam. One cannot refrain from drawing a parallel between the end of a postmodern mindset, cultural relativism, and the advent of debates over Islamic issues in the European public sphere; these debates called for ordering differences, establishing a hierarchy of values, and possibly even searching for Western hegemony over definitions of modern cultural values.

Let me narrow our angle further and pursue the notion of civilizational difference and how it made its way into the public debates of present-day Europe. The idea of Europe as a distinct civilization from Islam came to be expressed during the debates that started in 2002 over Turkey's candidacy for the European Union (EU). Turkey played a seminal role in prompting a public debate on European identity and cultural values. Until then European issues were mainly restricted to economic and political questions and were discussed within the political realm and negotiated with European bureaucrats. Likewise, the debate on Turkey's membership was considered to be a question of international politics, belonging to the domain of foreign affairs. However, in the space of a few years, issues over Turkish membership have mobilized public opinion, bringing the question of European identity and values to the foreground. In parallel to this shift, not only did the Turkish application for membership become part of domestic politics in European countries, but it also provoked a wider debate over the cultural and religious definitions of Europe, its frontiers, and its identity.

The very legitimacy of Turkey's membership in the EU was to be first questioned in France (and not in Germany where most Turkish migrants live). In 2002, Valéry Giscard d'Estaing, former president of France and then head of the European Union's Constitutional Convention, was the first to argue overtly against Turkish membership. In his opinion the acceptance of Turkey would mean the "end of Europe" as Turkey belonged to a "different culture, different mentality, and different way of living." His words expressed what many European politicians thought privately, as did also many private citizens.[6] This statement broke a taboo especially in France where republican universalism is esteemed to be a way of overcoming, and if necessary silencing, religious and cultural differences. The French republican secular heritage, referred to as French singularity (or French exceptionalism) is defended in many ways in opposition to the multiculturalism of the Anglo-Saxon tradition. Ironically, the arguments against Turkish membership brought the notion of civilization into public discourse, but with a semantic shift away from French universalism; it was a concept that resonated with Huntington's use, or the German notion of *kultur*.

The debate on Turkish membership turned into one about European frontiers and European identity. Whether Turkey belonged to Europe or not was discussed in different European contexts, in reference to differences in the geographical borders, historical heritage, and cultural values. The othering of Turkey was also meant to draw the boundaries of Europe and determine whether they were defined in geographical, historical, or religious, namely civilizational, terms.[7] Turkey as the only Muslim-majority candidate for the EU and a Muslim-migrant country crystallized in different ways the presence of Muslims both from within and outside Europe. Turkish membership was feared to be a "Trojan horse" that would carry Islam into Christian lands; it was perceived as a "forced marriage," one imposed by political elites but resented by European people; it would mean renouncing the victory of Europe over the Ottoman Empire in 1683 at the gates of Vienna. In sum, according to most Europeans, accepting Turkey into the EU would mean blurring

European identity and extending its frontiers toward the dangerous East.

A second move toward redefining European identity can be located in regard to the debates over its Christian roots. A tacit equation between Europe and Christianity has been expressed more and more overtly in recent public debates. Pope Benedict XVI in his widely quoted speech at Regensburg in 2006 argued that Christianity, contrary to Islam, is a religion of reason and invited European intellectuals not to dismiss the Christian spiritual sources in defining European identity. The Pope claimed that, in contrast to Islam, the tradition of Christian faith has the virtue of using reason and cherishing rational values: a tradition that stems, in his view, from the harmony and the "inner rapprochement between Biblical faith and Greek philosophical inquiry."[8] As if responding to the Pope's invitation, we observe that a wide range of European intellectuals from different backgrounds have become more welcoming to religion and have turned toward the defense of Christian values. Whether or not there should be a reference to Christian values in the European Constitution was the subject of intense debate among the member countries of Europe before it was refuted by the leadership of France. Turkish candidacy has thus exacerbated the ambivalent relation between secular definitions and the Christian roots of European identity.

These examples enable us to depict the changing self-presentation of Europeans in their encounters with the different aspects of Islam. European self-presentation is based on a discourse of civilization, but the notion of civilization changes from claiming to be universal to being particular, a European distinctiveness. The question of difference, whether it is religious, cultural, or ethnic, is framed in a discourse about civilization and in an attempt to draw boundaries with Islam. By Islam, I am not referring here to a historical, theological macroentity, but to the controversial ways Islam enters European societies: Turkish EU candidacy, the French headscarf debate, honor killings in Germany, the Danish cartoon controversy, the assassination of the filmmaker Theo van Gogh in the Netherlands, and al-Qaeda attacks in Madrid, London, and Istanbul. These are different acts and deeds in different national settings, but each refers to a controversy involving Islam in Europe. These controversies have engendered a series of conceptual debates ranging from veiling to martyrdom, from gender equality to violence, from freedom of expression to blasphemy. All contribute to the different ways in which Islam is anchored in the European public sphere, memory, and legislation, leading to a more general debate on the cultural values of Europe.

Islam—which was once thought to be a ghostly presence from the past, a relic expected to fade away with the process of modernization and secularization—today comes onto the stage of contemporary Europe. As a result of immigration and globalization, the issues over Islam are not confined to one geographic space, such as the Middle East, or to a Muslim-majority nation-state like Turkey or Iran, but have become part of European reality. The presumed time lag in modern discourse between those who are advanced and those who lag behind disappears. The geographical separation between those who are considered to be civilized and the rest ceases to reassure. The initial question, "What time is it there?," evoked at the beginning of this chapter, pointed to the differences in time zones and to the geographical distance, which now disappear. Europeans and Muslims have become close to one another in the same time zone and share—not always willingly and with the same desires—the same public spheres, schools, politics, and daily life. The notion of civilization enters present-day European politics where time lag and geographical separation between peoples and civilizations no longer apply.

Theories of Orientalism and postcolonialism have helped us to frame the question of difference between the West and the Oriental world in terms of domination, between the power of the colonizer and the colonized subordinate, between the majority and minority groups.[9] The critiques of Orientalism dealt with the ways in which the distant or exotic Other was constructed by the dominant Western discourses and imaginations. Postcolonial theories brought to our attention (as the prefix *post* encapsulates) the histories of the past that had been discarded and suppressed by colonial narratives. Multiculturalism posed a challenge to the monocultural foundations of the nation-state, bringing race and gender issues and majority and minority rights into the political realm. However, neither multicultural politics nor postcolonial approaches or Orientalist critiques fully capture the present-day European Muslim migrant history. Multiculturalism refers to the question of difference as an identity issue but dismisses issues of agency, social interaction, and ambivalence. Postcolonialism describes the power relations stemming from a particular historical experience, that of colonialism. Even though postcolonial history underpins the different national modes of encounter in present-day

Europe, such as the one between France and Algerians, Britain and Indians, the history of migration in Europe is not exclusively that of postcolonialism. In this respect, the relationship between Germany and the migrant Turks, which is not linked to a colonial past, is significant in drawing on the novel features of the encounter. In present-day discourse the representation of the Other has shifted from the distant unknown Oriental to that of Muslims living in proximity with Europeans and perceived as threatening intruders. The political revival of Islam has transformed European perceptions of Muslims and has also transferred the study of Islam from classical Orientalism to political science. The notion of Orientalism no longer suffices to describe the public depictions and meanings of contemporary Islam. While the presence of Muslims in Europe is not a recent phenomenon, and Europeans have had a long relationship with the Islamic world, the way that Europeans and Muslims become aware of one another's presence, confront their differences, and debate the aesthetic and ethical dimensions of modernity is a contemporary challenge. We need to elaborate a new analytical framework to bring out the dynamics of cultural confrontation in spatial proximity, a process that provokes, in spite of the asymmetrical relations of power and desire, a two-way exchange between Muslims and indigenous Europeans.

A process of cultural intermingling takes place. However, instead of leading to a peaceful coexistence, this has given rise to a series of antagonistic debates and events, through which both sides are transformed. Elsewhere, I have tried to capture this process in terms of mutual interpenetration between Islam and Europe and highlighted its embodied, gendered, and violent dimensions.[10] The German translation of the title of my work on interpenetrations between Islam and Europe is *Anverwandlungen*;[11] it is an old word, seldom used in modern times, which well conveys the sense of change of the self and the other, the metamorphoses that proximity can cause. Indeed, the synchronic proximity between Muslims and Europeans engenders an antagonistic bond between the two that leads, albeit unintentionally, to the transformation of public culture. Muslims enter public spaces bringing issues that are considered to be anachronistic in European modernity, such as religion, Islamic covering of women, martyrdom, blasphemy, and violence. In turn, Europeans engage in relating to these issues in different ways, in diverse voices, and from different perspectives. There is a two-way transgression, mutual crossings of the symbolic and spatial boundaries that provoke anxiety, change, and violence. I shall try to illustrate the social choreography in question by means of studying a controversy over the statue of a woman.

172

Public Bodies and Spatial Transgressions

The controversy concerns a public sculpture, titled *Turkish-Delight*, a life-size bronze female figure, naked with a headscarf covering her hair. The sculpture is the work of a well-known German artist, Olaf Metzel. It was exhibited in front of the Kunsthalle Museum in Karlsplatz in Vienna in November 2007. Not surprisingly, the artwork failed to delight many members of the Turkish migrant community living in the city. For some, it was offensive to Turkish women or an affront to the national pride of the Turks and, for others, an insult to their religious values. Whether to defend gender, national, or religious identity, or all three at once, the Turkish community raised their voices and requested its removal. A few months later, the statue was wrenched from its pedestal and left lying on the ground in the public garden. Two men who damaged the statue were caught through the images of surveillance cameras. Though not officially identified, they were presumed to be members of the Turkish migrant community. After all, the statue's title, *Turkish-Delight*, made it clear that it was addressed to the Turkish community and not to Muslim migrants in general. Later a young member of one of the most influential business families in Turkey discreetly bought the statue for his private art collection and museum in Istanbul. His gesture can be read as a desire to remedy the act of intolerance of his fellow Turks but also as a "performative" act (possessing the undesired object). Not only did he endorse the defense of the freedom of artistic expression but also silently and nondiscursively took part in the public debate that followed the removal of the sculpture.

After the forcible removal of *Turkish-Delight* from its garden, Vienna's Kunsthalle Museum housed an exhibition that took place from January 24 to March 16, 2008. It was called "Footnotes on Veiling: *Mahrem*."[12] The exhibition came to Vienna from Istanbul, from the Santralistanbul artspace in Bilgi University. This exhibition was a continuation of the headscarf issue but with a broader perspective on public-private distinctions and included works by mainly female artists from different national backgrounds—Iranian, Turkish, Algerian, Syrian, Portuguese, both Muslim and secular—living in different cities in the Middle East and Europe. It was meant to initiate an intercultural way of looking at things and to pursue the public debate in a new, introspective manner. In the words of a Muslim member of the Viennese community, the mahrem exhibition provided a veil for, and covered the nudity of, the *Turkish-Delight* statue. This was not intended. Yet it meant that the exhibition brought to mind the sense of interiority from a gendered perspective and entered into communication with the previous exhibition, namely the naked statue, while adding a new layer to the public debate. This communication illustrates the role of transnational dynamics and cultural mobility in shaping the European public sphere. The latter is emerging in debating ways of inhabiting space, ways of separating interior and exterior spaces, and differentiating the values of the sacred from the profane. The effect of cultural mobility and transnational circuits is to link different cultures and past memories together in many different and competing ways. European public culture emerges as a result of these multilayered juxtapositions and competing constellations.

The artworks themselves followed a transnational circuit and brought different peoples and nations into contact; the *Turkish-Delight* statue was first created and exhibited in Germany, and then in Vienna, and now remains in Istanbul (if it is ultimately exhibited in Turkey, one wonders what meanings it will take on in a nonmigrant context). The *Mahrem* exhibition opened in Istanbul, moved to Vienna and later to Berlin, to the two cities that are particularly important in Ottoman-Turkish history. The exhibition reversed the direction of the flow of art, shifting the center from European cities to Istanbul. Not only did the artworks and exhibitions circulate among different publics and gain different meanings, but also different national publics were brought into contact with each other by means of these controversies. The headscarf issue, in crossing the geographical frontiers and private-public boundaries, ceased to be a Muslim-Muslim concern and became a concern for all, a public issue for Europeans. Furthermore, controversies over gender, body, and space bring materiality of culture and visual difference to the public eye. The domain of art and in particular of visual art is becoming the preferred domain in which these controversies are revealed and shaped insofar as it captures the pictorial, corporeal, and spatial dimensions of these conflicts.

The public sphere, which is meant to provide through art, the sciences, and politics a shared space, a sense of commonality among citizens, becomes a realm of conflict and confrontation. Many not only fear that Muslim migrants are failing to share the same values as European citizens, such as freedom of expression, pluralism, autonomy of artistic domain, and gender equality, but moreover that, in the name of religion, they are intimidating, by use of force, those who want to exercise and live in conformity with these values. This leads to a totalizing discourse on Islam that associates religion with issues of migration, gender, and terrorism. As a result, "Anti-immigrant xenophobic nativism, secularist antireligious prejudices, liberal-feminist critiques of Muslim patriarchal fundamentalism, and the fear of Islamist terrorist networks are being fused indiscriminately throughout Europe into a uniform anti-Muslim discourse."[13] Casanova argues that a discourse of this type on Islam recalls the nineteenth-century discourse on Catholicism, depicted as an essentially antimodern, fundamentalist, illiberal, and undemocratic culture.

For many the incommensurability of the two cultural worlds

is so great that it is feared Islam will undermine the pillars of European public life. On the other hand, Muslims resent the way they are (over)represented by their religion; all migrants are not religious, and as many would assert, they adhere to secular values of freedom and equality. Furthermore, many regret that since 9/11 (a date that occurs frequently in the discourse of European Muslims) no difference is made between pious Muslims and radical Islamists, and Islam is too easily coupled with violence and terrorism, offending many and leading to *cultural racism*[14] against Muslim migrants, and even to *Islamophobia*, a newly coined notion that captures the emotional, irrational substratum of the totalizing discourse on Islam.[15]

Normative arguments, linear readings, preference for one group rather than the other, being provocative or being offended, choosing between freedom of expression and dignity will not help to capture the dynamics of cross-interpretations of the new cultural politics. Let us rather fix our gaze on the statue and engage in a two-way reading to tease out the several possible and conflicting interpretations from the two different—Turkish and Austrian/German—cultural perspectives. The statue depicts a Turkish woman, a Muslim (the headscarf symbol) alone in the midst of a public garden at the center of Vienna. It conveys a sense of vulnerability. By exposing a Muslim woman's uncovered body to public view, to masculine gazes, the statue contradicts Islamic prescriptions. Women who cover their heads do so to convey a sense of piousness and sexual modesty. They communicate to male members of the community a regime of social interaction that is meant to avoid physical contact, including eye contact, considered sinful (*göz zinası*) in Islam. The exposure of the statue of the woman to male eyes, including those of non-Muslims, is a transgression of religious prescriptions and provokes a displacement of the meaning of the veil.

Nudity has different cultural and religious connotations in different contexts. A woman naked in the midst of a natural landscape can be read as a return to the state of nature and thus as a sign of innocence from the point of view of the German heritage of naturalism. But from the point of view of Islam, covering certain parts of one's body (a prescription for both men and women) is a sign of the ability to control one's instincts, to discipline one's self and desires (*nafs*), and marks a difference in standing from others, such as naked slave women. The nudity of the *Turkish-Delight* statue is provocative because it works against the purpose of the headscarf, which is a reminder of Islamic distinction, religious piety, and feminine morality. By using both nudity and covering, the artist plays one against the other and introduces contradictions with Islam and with Muslim women's assertions of sexual modesty and social distinction.

However, in the case of the *Turkish-Delight* statue, the nudity of the female does not seem to invite seduction or sexual provocation. The nonexpressive face, the motionless body, and the dark skin (the bronze) remind us of the photographs of North African women taken by European artists, the colonial representations of women, their naked breasts conveying a state of nature and primitiveness in comparison with Western civilized women. One can interpret it as Western male eyes trying to subordinate and demystify Islam by undressing a woman's body, appropriating and assimilating it to the colonized subordinate (noting, though, that being portrayed as subordinate is foreign to Turkish imagery as they were themselves colonizers).[16]

One can also read an Orientalist gesture in the linking of the *Turkish-Delight* with a woman. The popular age-old Turkish sweet *loukoum*, produced since the fifteenth century, captures the image of the Oriental bazaar and its sensual pleasures. The sweet taste of loukoum (made from starch and sugar), its soft, jellylike, sticky consistency, its flavors such as rosewater or mint, and the pieces of hazelnuts, pistachios, or walnuts in the small cubes is a mouthful symbolic of Oriental opulence. Turks themselves use the label *loukoum* to describe beautiful, sweet, and attractive women. The statue of the woman does not capture the sensuous and charming sense of beauty that Turkish loukoum might evoke. Here again the statue introduces an anachronism both with the Turkish sense of beauty as well as the Orientalist representations of women. The statue is far from being a reproduction of the Orientalist images of women: living in the interior of a harem, lying on a sofa and assisted by a black eunuch, playing the lute, as depicted by Jean-Auguste-Dominique Ingres in his famous painting, *Odalisque with a Slave*. The Orientalist vision tried to penetrate and conquer the mysterious interiors of the Oriental Turkish harem, whereas the statue breaks away from both the exotic interior and the erotic Other, the pillars of Orientalism. In the case of the *Turkish-Delight* sculpture, the opulence and luxury of the Orient are replaced by the image of working-class peasant migrants; here we have the familiar Other, nearby, in proximity, in the public square. All exotic mystery and erotic attraction are gone.

Likewise migrants find themselves outside their Oriental home and its protections. The statue is not exhibited in the interior space of the Kunsthalle Museum but outside, in front of the building in the public garden. It follows women in their mobility as it steps out from interior and sacred spaces (mahrem) into the exterior space of public life. Migrant Muslim women are covered, yet they are publicly visible (or more precisely, they become visible because they are covered). The statue captures the status of migrant women in European cities. Quite unlike what one might imagine with respect to migrant Muslim women's real lives, the *Turkish-Delight* statue-woman is alone; there are no children, no female or male family members who accompany her. Contrary to the common representations of Muslim women, who are thought to be under the authority of the male members of the community, the statue draws on the isolation of the migrant woman. It represents the true condition of a migrant woman, vulnerable and uprooted, in a foreign environment without family support, and in the midst of a public garden, in the open air, in a European city. The public space where she is standing, motionless and lost, provides a sort of mental collage between her village peasant background and the natural surroundings of the public garden, suggesting that she has not yet found her way into European city life.

Muslim women themselves unsettle and transform the symbolic meanings of the Islamic covering insofar as they have transgressed the traditional boundaries of home and country and entered into secular life-spaces that were not initially intended for them. The spatial transgression of the veil challenges both traditional Muslim conceptions as well as secular feminist ones. By being personally covered and publicly pious, Muslim women expose a sense of agency that works against the Orientalist representations of women of the interior as well as the Westernist representations of secular feminism. What is at stake, therefore, is the reconfiguration of the migrant Muslim women in the European landscape. The statue exemplifies the tensions of this reconfiguration caught between past and present as well as between conflicting symbolic orders. It reflects the ways in which European publics and, in this case, the German sculptor are struggling and engaging with the Islamic headscarf of women in particular and with Islam in general. The aesthetic realm as an interactive space between art and politics, between cultures and publics, participates in the elaboration of a bond (which also includes elements of provocation and violence) between Muslims and Europeans.

One needs to track down how, at the present time, at ground level, by means of micropractices, different cultural perspectives and social groups meet with each other, confront their differences, and make them public. The notion of a European public sphere does not refer here to an entity already in existence, constituted by the extension or the addition of different national publics, but to the process of its making. The confrontational issues over Islam provoke debates on cultural values, mobilize collective passions, bring forth new voices and faces, follow transnational dynamics, and create overlapping public spaces.

From the Kunsthalle Public Garden to
European Public Constellations

The public garden exemplifies at microlevel the public sphere
at large. Whereas the public sphere tends to be conceptualized in abstract terms and in relation to a nation, with a language community and citizenship rights, the public garden
displays the physical and spatial aspects of the public square,
which comprise a plurality of perspectives. It enables us to
situate the controversy in space, bringing forth the visual and
performative aspects, and extending our notion of public beyond those who are recognized as public citizens sharing the
same language community. The statue is addressed not exclusively to Viennese residents, but to all: migrants and Muslims,
men and women living in the city, but also Turks living outside
the city. The statue provoked a public divide, an intercultural
(mis)communication, and a bond between diverse players and
diverse publics, not always sharing the same definition of national public. The statue itself exemplified the way the German
artist saw and depicted covered migrant women and the way
the two were coming to terms with each other. Paradoxically,
the statue made public certain issues and people, assembled
and interrelated by means of a confrontation following transnational and intercultural dynamics.

The spatial quality of the public sphere and the plurality
of perspectives are stressed in the work of Hannah Arendt.
As Christian Geulen argues, in Arendt's approach one finds a
notion of the public explicitly avoiding the presupposition of
symmetry; "a common world disappears when seen under one

aspect; a common world only exists in the variety of perspectives."[17] Hence public space is made up of, and constituted by and through, the articulation of different perspectives. Arendt insists on the notion of a concrete public space (*Öffentlicher Raum*) rather than an abstract one (*Öffentlichkeit*) and the special role of physical, corporeal difference in public: "in public space, where nothing counts but to be seen and to be listened to, visibility and audibility are of major importance."[18] Arendt elaborates the notion of public space as a communal space of visibility where citizens are able to meet with one another, confront each other so that they can examine an issue from a number of different perspectives, modify their views, and enlarge their position to incorporate that of others. First of all, public space is a plurality of perspectives. That is why Arendt rarely refers to, except to criticize, the concept of public opinion, which presupposes a common mass point of view for all. Second, the *polis* for Arendt is the space where individuals make their visibility explicit to each other. But the specificity of this public space is that it does not survive the fleeting instant. "Wherever people gather together, it is potentially there, but only potentially, not necessarily and not forever."[19] This type of public space of visibility can always be re-created wherever individuals gather politically. Since it is a creation of action, this space of visibility is highly fragile and exists only when materialized through the performance of deeds or the utterance of words.[20] But by means of narratives (she says that was why the Greeks valued poetry and history so highly), the memory of deeds can be preserved and passed on to future generations as a repository of instruction. The nature of the political community is therefore also a community of remembrance.

To recapitulate, the public sphere is constituted by the plurality of perspectives; it is the space where individuals make their appearance explicit to one another by means of performance and action; it is the product of the fleeting instant, namely it is not fixed once and for all but inhabited by action, conflict, and confrontation; narratives inscribe the ephemeral nature of events in the memory of the political community. Drawing on these aspects, I wish to stress first the importance of space as a physical locality that enables individuals to meet each other face to face; second, the performative dimension of action alongside the discursive one; and third, the cultural struggles over memory and visibility in the emerging European (and Islamic) public spheres. A public sphere can be conceptualized as constituting of public constellations in which the plurality of cultural perspectives meet with each other, but also collide, where individuals make their differences and appearances explicit to each other, not only by discursive arguments but also by performative practices, ranging from visual art forms (as in the case of the statue), architecture (construction of mosques), fashion (veiling), and the market (leisure and consumption patterns).

The Role of Islam as an Amplifier

The question of cultural difference, as it is conveyed by Islam in the European public sphere, calls therefore for a conceptual adjustment of the hermeneutics of the public sphere. First, there is an element of exacerbation in making oneself explicit to the other. Cultural and religious differences are made to be audible, visible, and demonstrative. Islam acts as an amplifier for both

Muslims and non-Muslims who use it as a reference. Thus, the use of the Islamic headscarf made the *Turkish-Delight* statue more visible and scandalous, thereby extending its public perception. But it was not the simple presence of the religious symbol that made the statue more public. The religious reference was exacerbated by means of a transgressive gesture (nudity), which provoked scandal and controversy.

The contemporary phenomenon of Islamic veiling is also an outcome of a form of exacerbation of religious difference. Young Muslim women embrace religion in ways that are different from the previous generations; they differentiate themselves as educated and self-aware Muslims in opposition to their mothers or grandmothers who, in the eyes of their daughters, reproduce unquestioningly the traditional ways of religious transmission and practices. Islam becomes a more explicit reference for pious self-fashioning, and the new generation of urban and educated Muslims interprets the head-covering in more literal terms; they replace the loose headscarf of their mothers by adopting new modes of covering their hair entirely. The headscarf becomes a hyperbole in making religious difference explicit to others. The semantic shifts in the debates—from the label "headscarf" to "Islamic veiling" and "hijab"—illustrate this move from a traditional quasi-invisible sign to that of the affirmation of cultural-religious difference. But once again it is not the simple presence of the religious symbol but its spatial transgression that makes it (over)visible and controversial. Muslim women literally cross the borders, moving by means of migration from small towns and villages to big cities, to European countries. The present-day head-covering becomes visible to the public eye to the extent that it penetrates deep into the nerve centers of secular modern life-spaces, such as schools, universities, and cities, but also becomes part of (street) fashion, consumption patterns, and political discourse.

Contemporary head-covering is neither a continuity of traditional religious prescriptions nor assimilation to the secular modern. Traditional religious groups, and also secular modernist people, expect a covered Muslim woman to be confined to a private space, to a given role, and not conspicuous to the public eye. On the other hand the neoveiling of women who thereby choose to be personally pious while advancing in public life (education, profession, politics) destabilizes both the traditional prescriptions of modesty and secular feminist norms of emancipation. Resorting to neoveiling—a practice that was supposed to hide, silence, and segregate women—renders Muslim women more public, visible, and controversial. It provokes a general debate on the place of religion in public life, on issues such as religion and agency, freedom of choice and veiling, and equality of faith and gender. As it becomes part of the public debate in Europe, it ceases to be exclusively an issue among Muslims (traditional versus radical, Islamist men and covered girls); it challenges secular cultural values and self-presentation of Europeans, men and especially women.

Post-1968 secular feminism made public the personal-private domain that stood in their eyes for women's oppression, as the slogan "the personal is political" conveys. It worked against the power of religion over women and released women's bodies from religious prescriptions (in fighting for abortion and contraceptive rights) and puritan morals and clothing (the removal of the corset as an emblem of bodily constraints). Secular feminism liberated women from a set of religious and conservative constraints and introduced a new set of practices in conformity with the rhetoric of emancipation. Women's bodies became salient, if not decisive sites where women anchored their identities and employed their strategies of liberation. Today, a modern woman makes her emancipation explicit (and apparent) in diverse exploits of body—embracing sexual autonomy, physical fitness, beauty and fashion, new-age health, and the like. If for the secular woman the possibilities for women's liberation are thought to be opened up by means of owning one's body, for pious women, there is an element of abstraction from the body. Seen through the lenses of modern life, veiling can be read as conveying a dual meaning and criticism—both religious and moral. First, as a reminder of God's will and presence in profane life, ideally veiling is a form of resistance (although in practice many veiled women desire to follow the commercial patterns of beauty and leisure) to the spiral of secular aesthetic and materialistic exploits of the body. Second, veiling displays a grammar of Islamic feminine identity that is based on covering and hiding parts of a woman's body and therefore is a reminder of the sacred, secret, gendered domain (which is both spatial and corporeal), that is, protecting the mahrem while being in public.[21] Here again this is an ideal situation because young covered women are faced with many contradictions and do think about the tensions that arise from their commitment to norms of modesty and their desire for participation in public life.[22] Nevertheless, the secular and Islamic approaches do exemplify two different and opposite modes of management of sexuality and femininity in public life. Islamic women become public by covering their hair and controlling their desires, while the grammar of emancipation calls for women to be accessible. These two different approaches to self-presentation in public life appear to be incommensurable. Adopting a Western style in the public sphere enables an opening for the possibilities of exchange (including being seen) and multiple encounters, while providing a space for anonymity and a space for "stranger sociability." Michael Warner argues that one of the defining elements of modernity is normative stranger sociability. He writes: "In modern society, a stranger is not as marvelously exotic as the wandering outsider would have been in an ancient, medieval, or early modern town. . . . In the context of a public, however, strangers can be treated as already belonging to our world. More: they *must* be. We are routinely oriented to them in common life. They are a normal feature of the social."[23]

However, the Islamic sense of intimacy and modesty works against the modern stranger sociability; the daily practices of gender segregation, the covering of women, the supervised communities (*mahalles*), and the inward-looking architecture are such examples.[24] An Islamic form of self-presentation requires the limitation of the public self by evoking the sacredness of the interior space and women's mahrem, gendered spaces, and covered bodies. Meanwhile, paradoxically, both the secular and the Islamic bring matters of sex and public life to the center of political debate. They are mirror images of each other.

Through this process, those who are not thought to belong to the same group (such as secular feminists and Islamic women, migrants and residents, Muslims and Europeans) are brought into close proximity with each other and create a new public constellation. Western notions of secularism, feminism, and art are revisited in their confrontation and encounter with Islam. Likewise Muslims find themselves confronting the differences between a lifestyle based on religious precepts and one of secular life experiences and reinterpreting the frontiers between the licit and the illicit in a Muslim-minority context. Issues around gender and sexuality are central, especially for the younger generation who are sharing a similar life experience with their European counterparts. They appropriate values of religious modesty and morality in a context where social mixing between men and women is inevitable; they have to face and discuss taboo topics such as the limits of friendship and flirting, virginity and marriage, and falling in love with a person of another religion.

Space matters: different places are subjected to public attention when religious, performative agencies challenge, contest, and reveal the unwritten laws of habitation and codes of interaction (also known as codes of civility). Hence communal spaces, such as schools, universities, hospitals, public gardens, public transport, working places, beaches, and swimming pools become public issues when an Islamic presence forcibly enters and disrupts the norms of the modus vivendi. Islam as a form of ethics and aesthetics disrupts European secular life spaces and modes of sociability. Hence the public sphere is not all about discursive communities, rational arguments, truth, and assertions of validity among citizens of a national community. The material, visual, pictorial, and sensorial dimensions of public communication and social confrontation become salient and decisive, thus provoking a politics of emotion.

There is a strong presence of an emotional stratum, which is heightened by the visual, pictorial dimensions of the controversies that ensue when technologies of communication ensure rapid circulation and reproduction among different publics. A transnational circuit provokes an emotional excess of cultural politics, as Michael Fischer has argued in relation to the Danish cartoon controversy.[25] These controversies occur in different places, at different times, and mean different things to different national publics, yet they create overlapping spaces, bringing together things, people, and ideas in new public constellations. The Salman Rushdie affair, the headscarf debate, the assassination of Theo van Gogh, the Danish cartoon controversy—these are all constellation events that destabilize the relations of proximity with and distance from Islam, operate religious and spatial transgressions, and manage visual, pictorial dimensions of performativity (including violence). New public constellations are constituted by transnational dynamics and become autonomous in relation to the social interactivity in national spheres. Arjun Appadurai argues that by means of media technologies and migration flows the "global modern" produces different interactive contexts from those that are bound to a nation-state; he offers "ethnoscapes, mediascapes, technoscapes, financescapes, and ideoscapes" as a new way of mapping a postnational world.[26] He argues for an understanding of diversity beyond the multiplicity of different and distinct ethnicities, identities, and cultures and depicts a process of interactive and overlapping dimensions of the global, which implies that in some instances different ethnicities can meet in the same ethnoscape. This applies to my understanding of the public constellations in which distant and distinct people, ethnicities, ideas, and things come into close interaction and confrontation. The Salman Rushdie affair can be considered as being a *momentbilder* of a public constellation that brought the domain of aesthetics and Islam, as well as Europeans and radical Islamism, into close interaction and confrontation; it was followed by other such instances that took place in different parts of Europe, such as the Muhammad cartoons in Denmark, or the *Turkish-Delight* statue in Austria. The latter did not attain the velocity and intensity of those listed above; it remained relatively circumscribed without extending the boundaries of controversy and confrontation. Yet it is part of the new mapping of European constellations. It reveals the realm of aesthetics as an interactive space between different cultural subjectivities and politics, which appears to be pivotal in the making of European public constellations.

The European public sphere cannot therefore be studied as the addition and extension of national public spheres but as the formation of public constellations that bring together the unexpected and the incommensurable. We cannot clearly define the contours of this European public sphere nor can we speak of it as an established entity with defined norms and values. It is an ongoing process at the present time but should not be thought of as following a linear path of development. There is something sporadic, accidental, and at times violent in the making of European public constellations. It cannot be fully rendered through institutional, representative, organized politics, nor by studying uniquely the intention of the actors whether they are political elites or citizens; it is through the dynamics of interaction, encounter, conflict, and mutual transformation, namely through the unintended consequences of a series of beliefs and practices, events and controversies, that a European public sphere is taking shape. A number of apparently unrelated events, separated in time and in space, are linked to each other, creating a new form of mapping, a new pattern, forming a constellation in the sense described by Walter Benjamin.[27] For Benjamin, who was critical of the linear conception of history, modernity is not a one-way pendulum but should be approached as a dynamic and relational interpretation of history, of which the most appropriate image is a constellation.[28] Constellations bring together seemingly unrelated events separated in time and space and therefore create a new space of interpenetration and collision, which affects the course of change and meanings of the modern. The encounter between Europe and Islam is being shaped in a series of controversies and confrontations in the public sphere, which reveal the ways the two are entering into interaction, conflict, and mutual borrowings, creating thereby new constellations. These constellations incorporate the paradoxical combination of the two, challenging established narratives that describe European modernity and Islam as mutually exclusive, distinctive, and fixed entities.

8 Europe's Trouble with Islam

What Future?

The project of European Union is losing its appeal for European citizens themselves and developing in a direction that is diametrically opposite to the founding fathers' ideal of peace and pluralism. Europe's encounter with Islam is decisive. The general resentment against Turkish candidacy and the success of neopopulist movements in the elections for the European Parliament are signs that indicate the problem Europeans have with Islam.

In 2001, when I moved from Istanbul to Paris, I was not expecting that the European Union was going to enter into my area of interest. It is not that the European project did not matter to me until then. It did, in a similar way that it mattered to the majority of my friends and colleagues, Turkish and Kurdish intellectuals, from both secularist and religious backgrounds. At that time, our interest in Europe was mainly a Turkey-centered concern, derived from a widely shared expectation and desire that the EU would provide a political and juridical framework to enlarge and enforce the institutionalization of democratic rights and freedoms in Turkey. Europe was standing, in the minds of many progressive intellectuals, for a fulfilled prophecy of secular democracy, as a stable and fixed point of reference to promote the transformation of other societies. No one was expecting Europe to be transformed and shaped by its encounter with the issues related to Islam.

I was working on contemporary Islam, its emerging force and visibility in public life, and Turkey was my privileged terrain of observation. Turkey provided a site for studying Islamic movements in a politically pluralistic and secularist context. The pluralism implied a field of competing forces among political parties, social movements, and "truth regimes." Islamism had to compete among these different sets of ideas and powers. It was not appropriate therefore to speak of Islamization in Turkey, as it was widely framed for other Muslim-majority countries, in the sense that Islamism was increasingly taking over political power and gaining influence in all spheres of life and imposing itself as a single truth regime.

The study of Islam in Turkey differed from other Muslim-majority countries that were under monarchic authoritarian rules. In many respects, the place of Islam in Turkey, because of the secular legislation and a pluralistic political sphere, revealed some similarities with the European contexts of pluralism. Islamic claims—especially young female students' protests to wear a headscarf in university classes—caused a long-term public confrontation with those who were holding to republican principles of secularism and feminism. When the French headscarf debate, which had already started in 1989, took on a new momentum and magnitude in spring 2003, I was struck by the parallelisms with the Turkish one. The similarities between the two headscarf debates turned my attention to the ways in which French republican values of secularism and feminism were reshaped in relation to Islam and addressed against the claims for visibility of religion in the public sphere.

Perhaps no other social issue provoked more passion and debate in France than the Islamic headscarf in the public schools (a debate that peaked during the fall of 2003). This was followed by a debate over Turkish membership in the EU. These two long-lasting and nationwide debates culminated in, respectively, the passing of new legislation to ban the Islamic headscarf from public schools and a call for a referendum vote on Turkish membership. Two very distinct claims by Muslims—to wear a headscarf in secular public schools and for Turkish membership in the EU—thus triggered broader debates over the value of both secularism and European identity. The headscarf debate touched on issues of immigration, the secular public school system, the definition of citizenship, and the national politics of integration. However, Turkish membership in the EU cannot be equated with problems of migration (even less so in France than in Germany), nor can Turkey, which is a secular state, be identified with Islam. Yet, in public debates over the last two years, the matter of Turkish candidacy has shifted from the realm of foreign affairs to become a domestic issue that played a decisive role in the outcome of the referendum on the European constitution.

The Islamic headscarf issue created heated debates in France accompanied by an equally passionate and nationwide debate on the possibility of the Turkish presence in the EU and its consequences for European values and identity. It was by means of these two debates that the presence of Islam (Muslim migrants within Europe and Muslims outside the EU) was brought into the forefront of public concern and carried to public awareness. That is to say, the presence of Islam entered into the area of concern and debate for all citizens; it did not remain solely in the hands of the decision makers. Sociologically speaking, Islamic veiling and Turkish candidacy for the EU have little in common. They follow different historical trajectories. The veiling issue was related to the phenomenon of migration, the public schools, and gender equality. It was linked to new forms of religious agency stemming from contemporary Islamist movements. The Turkish candidacy for EU membership, however, is an outcome of a long-term history of westernization in Turkey. It was a result of political determination as well as societal mobilization to conform and frame Turkish society and its future with that of European unity. The agency that underpinned the Turkish demand for EU membership was a secular democratic one.

The scales of agency were equally different. Islamic veiling in France was a concern at a national level whereas the Turkish candidacy was debated at an international, European level. There were some bridges between the two affairs. Islamic veiling was being debated in Turkey as well. The question of Islam was (and still is) also addressed to Turkey, not only because it is a Muslim-majority country but also the government in power (AKP) was related to the Islamist movements of the 1980s that were contesting Western notions of democracy. These movements revealed the tensions between secular and religious orientations as well as the ongoing debate over the definitions of space. The public schools and Europe were becoming political spaces to the extent that they became a battleground for the re-definition of the frontiers of inclusion and exclusion and for the contestation of established values. The question of space points to the understanding and creating of "commonness," whether it is instituted by the public schools or the EU. Creating a common space with those who are external to national and European culture becomes a question whose answer goes beyond the one that is provided by the framework of integration. The intensity of the debate in the French public sphere illustrated the importance of the question, not only for outsiders and Muslims, but also and foremost for Europeans. The ways that these two issues were anchored in public consciousness and became part of the French and European public debate call for comparative attention.

Europe as subject matter imposed itself on me, but by a familiar gateway. Rather than leaving behind Turkey and Islam on moving to Paris, I was going to face and experience their presence in Europe. I moved to France, but I had the feeling that France also came closer to me by debating issues related to Islam and Turkey, the issues that were considered until then to be outside Western boundaries, and confined to the Middle Eastern culture and geography. When one moves to the West, one has the awkward habit of thinking that one is entering modern times and the land of innovation. However, I found myself in the midst of a debate with which I was already familiar in Turkey, as if history had been reversed and was running counterclockwise. One has the habit of measuring, for instance, the Turkish laïcité in the mirror of the French one and reading the deficiencies and gaps with the original. In the early 2000s, however, it was more meaningful to observe the French head-scarf debate in the mirror of the Turkish one. Well-known and widely circulated attributes of the Turkish laïcité can be summarized as the didactic aspect of secularism (teaching how to be civilized citizens) and the tendency toward authoritarianism and exclusionary politics (if necessary with the help of the military). There was also the feminist alliance with secular republicanism, an intrinsic feature of Turkish secularism that was going to become a salient feature of French secularism in its encounter with Islam. The comparison between the two head-scarf debates helped me to understand the French one in new ways. One can say that from the Turkish perspective, French laïcité ceases to be an exception, and the French headscarf debate presents itself as déjà vu. But in return, it becomes more and more difficult to translate and communicate the possible meanings of the French debate to the Turkish public. My interlocutors, especially the secularists, liberals, feminists, and pro-Europeans, found at first comfort and affinity in the secularist reaction of the French public to ban the headscarf from the public schools. They interpreted this radical stance as a proof of attachment to similar notions of laïcité and in addition as a sign of French-Turkish alliance. We observed the same celebration of the victory for Turkish secularists when the European Court of Human Rights in Strasbourg decided in November 2005 to support Turkey's ban on women wearing headscarves in universities.

The decision of the European court marked the end of a judicial battle that had started in 1988 when a Turkish student, named Leyla Şahin, who was barred from attending Istanbul

University medical school because of her headscarf, brought her case to the European court.[1] The European court decided to uphold Turkey's ban, on the arguments that Turkey treated men and women equally and that its constitution mandated a secular society. Furthermore, the court decision underscored that the notion of secularism in Turkey, which was seeking to join the EU, was consistent with the values underpinning the European Convention on Human Rights.

However, the majority of French intellectuals, feminists, politicians, or simple citizens did not think the same way as the European court. And those who were against the head-scarf in the public schools of France were also against Turkish membership in the EU. Turkish secularism seemed to matter for only a minority. This was difficult for Turks to understand. It was difficult for Europe-oriented democrats to comprehend the emergence of a strong public opinion in France, mobilized around nationalist, secularist, and feminist values and distinguished from migrants and Turks, who were perceived as Muslim "others."

One of the most often heard arguments was that French republicanism, criticized for its ethnic, racial, and religious blindness, was an exception and could not be generalized to other European countries. Although the French were fond of the republican and secularist values that they considered as the particularity of France, and they were willing to see Europe as French universalism written large, French republicanism was ill adapted not only to deal with a multicultural social reality but also to deal with the new realities of Europe in a global context. The French referendum vote against the European Constitution (May 29, 2005) can be taken as symptomatic of these insular and introverted dynamics. Although there was no obvious single reason for the rejection of the constitution, it translated to the fear and resentment of the French toward neoliberal globalization, enlargement of Europe, the Turkish question, and Muslim migrants, all reasons that made French citizens fear that their future, whether economic or political, was no longer in their hands and that they were no longer at home (*chez soi*) in their daily lives.

The two countries that have voted against the European constitution were the two countries where Islam was most debated publicly. Dutch society, though not driven particularly by secular republican ideals, felt the same. Three days after the referendum vote in France, the Dutch also rejected the European Constitution. In the Netherlands, politics of multiculturalism have led, in the eyes of many, to cultural separation and have failed to integrate Muslim migrants into Dutch society. The country witnessed an escalation of anti-immigrant and anti-Muslim resentments and politics in the early 2000s. Pym Fortuyn, an extreme right-wing and gay politician, who was gunned down by a radical environmentalist in 2002, had made the fight against immigrants and Muslims (whom he considered as inherently homophobic) the theme of his political campaign. In the same country, Somali refugee and MP Ayaan Hirsi Ali used her personal drama to access the political scene and to wage a cultural war against Islam. At the heart of her argument is the irreconcilable nature of Islam with liberal European societies, because of the abuses it supposedly imprints on women's bodies. Hirsi Ali collaborated with Theo van Gogh in 2004 to produce her film titled *Submission*, which uses the same narrative of women's subjugation within Islam: verses of the Quran on the naked bodies of women in agony, submitting to Allah despite their suffering, in a provocative staging of the Muslim woman as a failure of a psychocultural development.[2] On November 2, 2004, a few days after the release of the film, Theo van Gogh, a well-known public figure who personified the Dutch sense of freedom of speech, was assassinated in the middle of a street in Amsterdam by a young man of Moroccan origin.[3] Following this tragic event, Dutch public opinion expressed a stronger sense of commitment and the need for defending national values on the lines of Western culture against Islam. The incident brought into sharp focus the particular ways the encounter between Muslims and Europeans is unfolding in a pluralistic Dutch society, exposing the limits of a multiculturalist discourse.[4] No longer is a politics of cultural avoidance feasible, nor would it be desirable to draw boundaries between different communities marked by race, ethnicity, or religion. Yet anxiety is growing among both Muslims and Europeans about a perceived breakdown of boundaries, with a loss of identity that accompanies the dynamics of this encounter and is leading to the reinforcement of national and religious identities.

Both French republicanism and Dutch multiculturalism have been challenged by the ways Islam is Europeanized. Islam becomes European, and precisely because of this proximity, it engenders confrontation. It is in this phase of postimmigration integration that Islam emerges as a European issue. Muslim migrants are uprooted, distanced from their countries of origin, and acculturated, but their reterritorialization is linked in the public imagination either with a politics of terror (as in the case of the suicide bombers in the July 2005 attacks against London who were discovered to be British citizens) or with claims to religious visibility that conflict with fundamental European understandings of gender and citizenship. It seems that both the republican politics of integration and multiculturalist politics of difference fall short in face of the nonassimilative strategies of European Islam.

In France, the idea of maintaining boundaries and defending national identity became particularly pronounced in a series of public debates over the past two decades. Opposition to the Iraq War, criticisms of American policies, the status of the Islamic headscarf in public schools, and Turkish membership in the EU all provoked changes in the self-presentation of Europe as well as its representation of the other. The dissension around the Iraq War brought to light a fracture within the West, enhancing a definition of European values and politics opposed to the American quest for global hegemony. An anti-American attitude became part of the self-presentation of the French public and gave impetus to the mobilization of peace movements as a distinctive feature of European values.

The German legislative elections in September 2005 illustrated as well the extent to which issues around Islam, immigration, and Turkey's EU membership were becoming agenda-setting issues for internal politics. The leaders of the Christian Democrat Movement (Angela Merkel and Edmund Stoiber) captured the public attention and sympathy by overtly pronouncing their opposition to Turkey in the EU. Similarly in France, politicians who were orienting their politics to issues of security and taking a stand against Turkish membership (such as then minister of interior Nicolas Sarkozy, but also a marginal figure of the nationalist right in French political life, Philippe de Villiers, who made himself a place by his political campaign with the maxim "non à la Turquie") were gaining in popularity. After being elected as president in 2007, Nicolas Sarkozy hardened France's position on Turkey's admission to EU membership and declared on several occasions that he would not "tell French schoolchildren that the borders of Europe extend to Syria and Iraq."[5]

It is doubtful therefore to see these developments on the one hand in continuity with republican tradition, and on the other, as a uniquely French issue. Rather, we can argue that the claim of universalism underpinning French republicanism is in decline and the politics of nationalism are gaining ground, as in other European countries, in the face of encountering Islam. The discourse of integration, whether it is immigrant integration to host countries or Turkish integration to Europe, does not help to frame the two-way relation in this process. The discourse of integration calls for politics that would facilitate assimilation of the newcomers to the host culture and conform to the national order. But there is no place for understanding the two-way change that is already under way shaping both Muslims and Europeans and reducing the differences between these two categories. It is those social groups and generations that are in Europe, without hope for return, distanced from the national origins of their parents, shaped by new life experiences, European languages, public schools, and suburban districts of the European cities that negotiate their public visibility. Those who are transformed by these experiences claim both their difference and citizenship and signal the end of problematic migration. And the second and third generations do not identify themselves with their migrant origins. The French formula *issu de l'immigration* is felt as a stigma to the extent that they are determined by their parents' condition. In this respect, Islamic identity that young Europeans of migrant origin appropriate voluntarily marks the distance from the national origins of their parents. This newly appropriated Islam also expresses the wish to escape from the stigmatization that their parents were representing and transmitting to them: the Algerian colonial past in France or the image of the first generation, mostly illiterate Turkish guest workers (*gastarbeiter*), in Germany.

The headscarves of young Muslims exemplify the ways in which religious difference is carried into European publics, and ceases thereby to be confined to Muslim-majority nation-states, or to the Middle Eastern region. But in European contexts, veiling signals a change in the sociological and cultural profiles of the migrant, a change that can be broadly discussed in three stages of immigration. The first stage is marked by the figure of the immigrant, the solitary male worker, with a status of foreigner, temporary guest worker, gastarbeiter. The second stage is characterized by the settlement of the immigrant worker with his family. The figure of the "Arab boy" in France, for instance, is an outcome of this stage, representing second-generation youth who have no intention to return to their country of origin, yet who have not yet acquired the social credentials for integration into the host country. The Arab boy is perceived as a potential troublemaker, a deviant, with problems of education and unemployment.[6] Rather than in the factory, it was in the streets that one could have visualized the second generation migrant youth with street manifestations against racism signaled by the motto of "don't touch my friend" (*ne touche pas à mon pote*; the campaigns were visualized with the emblem of Fatima's hand). Whereas in the first stage, social problems inherent in the living conditions and legal status of workers are addressed, in the second stage, language learning and children's education become the priority for the politics of integration. Only in the third stage does the issue of religion become predominant. The new figure of the veiled Muslim girl at schools illustrates this new turn. The figure of the immigrant thus changes from the working-class male and the unemployed youth to young schoolgirls. Islam becomes an issue at this stage of postimmigration that links together categories of gender and religion.[7]

Hence the veil, originally meant to conceal femininity, brought migrant girls under public attention. The veil symbolized both the feminization and the Islamization of the migrant populations in Europe. The school became the battleground for the religious claims, but thereby revealed the presence of migrant girls and their greater level of integration through public education, compared to the previous generations. The headscarf of the young girls differs from that of the traditional female image of the first generation, of their mothers, mostly illiterate, homebound, uneducated, and dependent on their husbands. The daughters speak the language, whether it is French or German; they have access to public education but also to the grammar of communication and self-display in public. If the traditional headscarf of the first-generation Muslim migrants is not an issue, it is because the women who wear it are working class, living in their communities out of public sight, and do not claim to take a seat in the classrooms, circulate in urban life, or participate in public life. In contrast, the new generation of veiled schoolgirls is much more integrated and familiar with the culture of European societies. The Islam the schoolgirls appropriate is not the one from the countries of origin of their parents. Islam provides them with a way of escaping the original national culture that has little in common with their actual existence in European societies. They are in the process of reterritorialization and Europeanization; they come into public existence by turning their differences (even small ones) into public visibility, performed in everyday life by religious signs and rituals.

The sociological studies on migration depicted the marginalization of second-generation youth and their greater exposure to alienation, crime, drugs, or all sorts of radicalism, including terrorism. Integration follows different historical trajectories in different countries. French republicanism addresses a very high promise of integration, even that of assimilation. The German notion of citizenship, based on the notion of blood, does not claim to assimilate the other but is coupled with politics of indifference or cultural avoidance. The ties between Germans and Turks are less forceful; there is no colonial heritage that binds them through memory or through the language and the education system prior to waves of immigration. In other words Algerians are French in ways that Turks are not German. And furthermore, Turks are not expected or desired to become German.

Migrants and Muslims challenge the very places and vectors of integration and social mixing: the public schools, urban habitation, and public life. The public school is the pillar of the formation of citizenship in the republican French sense; in the school individuals are taught to distance themselves from their local attachments, class origins, regional accents, ethnic differences, and religious convictions in order to embrace universal knowledge and become French citizens. Apart from the schools, urban life also contributes to the making and learning of the bonds of civility, necessary for the politics of the *cité*. And the *laïque* conception of the public sphere is thought to provide neutrality; a space in the entrance of which particularistic identities, whether religious or ethnic, should be left behind, so that a conversation among equals (but one is not equally naked or stripped of one's differences) can take place. The presence of Muslims in public schools, in urban life, and in the public debate carries an undesired difference into the public sphere that claims to be difference-blind. Muslim presence in public also reveals the politics of putting the difference out of sight (as in the case of migrant-majority housings in *banlieues*), prohibiting it by law (as in the case of the headscarf) or labeling it as the "other," the foreigner. It is not the universalist claim but rather the equation between universal and French that creates a problem today. It is the ways that Western self-presentation holds to the hegemony over definitions of the universal. As Norbert Elias pointed out, the French culture, among other European cultures, was the one that contributed most to a universal (French and Western) understanding of civilization as opposed to the German notion of *Kultur*.[8] It is also in France where this equation is most noticeably challenged at present, where the encounter between Islam and Europe is displayed in the most dramatic way.

"Identifying" Europe means "Othering" Turkey?

The debates triggered by the Turkish candidacy to the EU exemplified the ongoing and unresolved encounter between the two, revealing the importance of the stakes that surpass the Turkish question and determine the future of Europe.

For Turks, it was a widely shared feeling that Turkey in joining the EU was to accomplish, somewhat naturally, the long historical course of Westernization that started in the late nineteenth century. European ideals had already shaped Ottoman reformist intellectuals, young Ottomans, and *jeunes turcs*, formed by the influence of French positivist thought and Jacobin tradition prior to the republican era. The foundation of the Turkish nation-state under the leadership of Atatürk in 1923 can be read as a culmination of this process, but the Atatürkist move was a radical step, almost as a civilizational shift, as a way of turning away from the heritage of the Ottoman Empire to embrace a new life and a new nationhood that will make Turkey part of the civilized nations.

However, from the point of view of the European nations, Turkish integration with the EU, although a process that was welcomed by European politicians in the past and started with the economic Ankara Agreement in 1963, did not seem to be that natural from the prism of present-day politics. Turkish candidacy became the most controversial issue after the meeting of the European Council in Copenhagen on December 12, 2002, to decide the calendar for opening negotiations with Turkey. The debate started in France where, unlike Germany, the Turkish immigrant population was not a major issue. It was Valéry Giscard d'Estaing, the former president of the French Republic and then president of the Convention on the Future of Europe, who initiated the heated debates on the entry of Turkey by bringing the argument of *difference* to the public agenda.[9] He claimed that "Turkey is not a European country, and its capital is not situated in Europe." For him, "Turkey belongs to those countries that make part of another culture, another way of life," and its integration into the EU would mark "the end of Europe." His arguments made their way into public opinion, found echo among politicians, intellectuals, and journalists, independent of their prior political views and differing convictions on other subjects. The Turkish issue ended up reshuffling political alliances and creating a new consensus among those who were until then in opposing camps and blurred the very deep divide between the left and the right in France. The number of articles published in the newspapers, the panels held on television programs, the emerging of public spokespersons, and the books on Turkey witnessed the intensity and the longevity of the debate that was carried into different spheres of public life, opening up a new market for publication and communication, but also for making politics. The boundaries of the public incessantly expanded from the mass media discussions, newspaper articles, and social scientific conferences to everyday life conversations taking place in marketplaces, at dinner tables, and among neighbors or strangers.

The arguments against Turkish membership in the EU did

not remain the same. The Turkish agenda of the 1970s was mainly determined by the violation of human rights, the repression of Kurdish nationalism, the influence of military power in Turkish political life, the discord with Greece over South Cyprus, and the official denial of Armenian genocide. But these questions, the "Turkish problems file," although they remained present, did not count for the arguments against Turkish candidacy. On the contrary, the debate started when the Turkish problems file was getting thinner, when Turkey started, as observers would put it, "to do her homework," to resolve some of the problems in order to fulfill the criteria for inclusion and become eligible for European membership. As Turkey edged closer to European criteria of democracy the arguments against Turkish membership were articulated and expressed in offensive, not to say aggressive, tones to the surprise of the Turkish pro-European democratic public.

One of the new arguments concerned the question of European territory. Turkey did not make part of European geography, let alone history, and threatened, in the eyes of many, the unity of Europe in geographical terms, representing an unlimited enlargement of frontiers. "Why not Morocco, and why not Russia?" were among the widely used arguments to denote the "absurdity" of Turkish membership. Including Turkey would have meant expanding the European borders toward the east, and becoming neighbors with those unwanted risk-countries. Another line of argument concerned more economic factors, basically the impoverishment of Europe by the already recent newcomers to Europe. Turkey appeared as a burden that Europe would not be capable of including into its system (in economic and political terms, Turkish membership in the European Parliament was feared to outweigh in numbers) without a high cost. Above all, Turkey was not a small country, and bringing more than seventy million Muslims into Europe would make a difference.

Questions of geographic frontiers, civilizational belonging, religious differences, and past memories all entered into the Turkish candidacy debate as a constellation of insurmountable differences and set a new agenda. Europe, until then an affair left in the hands of Eurocrats, became the center of a public societal debate, recomposing the political and intellectual arena independent of left-right, secular-religious, liberal-republican, or feminist-conservative divisions. Identifying with Europe meant othering Turkey. Opponents of the constitution (a coalition of both socialists and the nationalist right) used the Turkish candidacy in their campaign, establishing a forced equation between the two and implying that the rejection of the constitution would keep Turkey out of the EU. The rejection can be read as an indicator of the rise of nationalist sentiments and a defense of singularity, whether defined by French exceptionalism of integration and laïcité in a multicultural world, by social rights in a global liberal economy, or by French sovereignty against European solidarity.

The debate on Turkish EU membership became a concern for all when it started to be connected to the definitions of European frontiers, values, and future. Turkey became a catalyst, but also the other for what was to be defined as European. In that sense, othering Turkey became a way of identifying Europe. The need for an alterity to define European identity was integrated into the political discourse of those skeptical of Turkish membership in Europe. Turkey's entering Europe would mean, as Frits Bolkestein, the Dutch commissioner for the European Union, argued prior to entry talks with Turkey, "forgetting the importance of 1683, the date when the siege of Vienna was lifted and the Ottoman army was defeated." (One legend is that the croissant was invented in Vienna to celebrate the defeat of the Turkish siege of the city, as a reference to the crescent on the Turkish flags.) Hence the memory of the past entered into present-day cleavages and controversies. The objection of Austria, until the very last minute, to the opening of negotiations with Turkey on October 3, 2005, had something to do with past memories. (Austria agreed to remove its objections under the condition that Croatia also began membership talks.)

The opening of talks with Turkey was an important date, but it did not bring an end to the public debates or the processes of integration that would take decades. One should note an important shift that occurred in European politics and transferred the power of decision makers to that of opinion makers. The issues related with the EU that had been mainly in the hands of Eurocrats and resolved in Brussels moved to national publics and became part of societal debates. The idea of popular sovereignty that was extended and juxtaposed from nation-state politics to the EU illustrates this shift. The idea of a democratic Europe came to mean building Europe from below with the necessity of consulting people and a consensus on the need for referendums, whether to vote for the European constitution or for Turkish membership. The idea of a referendum was mostly defended by opponents of Turkish candidacy, counting on the popular vote for its rejection in ten years' time.

The European perspective forced Turkey to undertake a series of reforms that changed the republican definition of citizenship in order to be in harmony with democratic and pluralistic definitions of ethnic, political, religious, and individual rights. Turkish republicanism as the nation-state ideology was founded upon two pillars: secularism and nationalism, referred to as Kemalism. But these principles were also coupled with monocultural definitions of society, giving rise to antidemocratic interpretations of these principles, namely authoritarian secularism and assimilative nationalism. The working of the European project in Turkey meant the dismantling of the authoritarian and assimilative nature of republicanism.

Four concrete examples illustrate the ways in which Turkish society tried to overcome its authoritarian tendencies, breaking down taboo subjects and getting on a similar wavelength, not without inner tension and confrontation with European democracies. The first one was to overcome inbred tension between authoritarian secularism and democracy in the Turkish political system. We can speak of a vicious circle that can be seen in many other Muslim countries that were engaged with values of secularism and modernity, but at the expense of democratic pluralistic politics. Secularism in Turkey was implemented in the 1920s mainly by means of single-party authoritarian rules. Opening of a democratic space usually profits those who have been excluded and, in this case, the excluded ones were the Muslim groups searching for public recognition and political representation. To protect the secular state and the principles of the republic, the military power did not hesitate to put democracy into brackets. The Algerian parliamentary elections in 1992 were a dramatic example of such a dilemma; the Islamic Salvation Front (FIS) had the electoral victory, but the army dissolved the Parliament and canceled the elections in order to block Muslim fundamentalists' access to power. And in July 2013, the Egyptian army overthrew a democratically elected government of the Freedom and Justice Party of the Muslim Brotherhood, putting a check on the Arab Spring. In Turkey, the army occupied a central position in political life in its role as guardian of the secular republic. In the minds of democrats, there was a need to dismantle the army-backed secularism and create an inclusionary consensual secularism. This was possible only if there was a democratic space, shared both by the religious and the secular, the first giving up the absolutism of the religious truth-regime, and the latter giving up its claims of hegemony over society.

The AKP, which had Islamic roots, gained the 2002 general elections by democratic means and came to power in Turkey. We can speak of a buildup of democratic consensus between secular and religious publics, through an interactive process that transformed both parties. In that respect, what Jürgen Habermas describes as a cognitive precondition for a religious-secular dialogue was being engaged in Turkey. And furthermore, rather than being a mere discursive debate and a dialogue between two supposedly fixed identitarian groups, this interaction between the secular and the religious transformed Turkish society and opened up new intermediate spaces for consensus building.

In spite of the ongoing cleavages and conflicts between hard-liner Islamists and the secularist establishment, Turkish society experienced during two decades a "fall of the wall" that had separated and divided two Turkeys, one composed of educated urban and West-looking secularist upper and middle classes labeled as *white Turks* and the other faith-driven lower-middle-class *black Turks* originating from Anatolian towns.[10] The course of upward social mobility changed the life trajectories of many belonging to the latter group (turned them into *gray*, meaning partially whitened), who had access to higher education in the 1960s with emigration to urban cities, profited from new market opportunities that expanded in the 1980s, and invested in the avenues of political power since the electoral victory of the AKP. The thinning of the wall between the two faces of Turkey brought different publics and cultural codes in close contact and interaction, albeit with intense conflict, yet transforming the mutual conceptions of Muslim and secular publics and limiting the claims of hegemony of the latter. In the post-1980 period, the frontiers between the two publics became more porous and led spokespersons of Muslim, leftist, liberal movements to engage in public debates, to participate in roundtables, and to cross the borders of their own neighborhoods and address themselves to each other's publics. Well-known public intellectuals from the leftist movement started to write in conservative religious or radical Islamic newspapers (*Zaman* or *Yeni Safak*), while those from the Islamic movement turned their attention to secular publics and media (as in the case of Ahmet Hakan, the popular anchorman of the Islamic TV channel, who became a columnist in the secular mainstream daily *Hürriyet*). Such success-driven transpublic crossings were unthinkable prior to the1980s. These crossovers helped to establish bridges of dialogue between divided publics and created a new mental space for thinking and linking the two faces of Turkey, secular and Muslim, in a more interactive way that generated mutual transformation.

The democratic sphere gained momentum to the extent that the polarization between the secularist and Islamist publics was played down, leading to an intermediary space of debate and representation. In this context the European perspective reinforced the democratic momentum and created a new political agenda of reform. The mobilization of human rights movements in civil society, the formation of a public opinion in favor of these reforms, and the determination of the government and the political classes all culminated in a series of reforms that were passed by parliamentary vote during the course of 2002–3 in order to harmonize the Turkish legal system with the Copenhagen criteria.

Second, the abolition of the death penalty was a major example illustrating Turkish society's democratic efforts, embracing a widely shared societal value in Europe, in contrast to American society. The Turkish Parliament voted in favor of abolishing the death penalty on August 2, 2002, a first in a Muslim country. The repercussions it had for Turkey were far more than just to please Europeans, as cynical observers argued. The project of abolition of capital punishment deepened the political divide and confrontation with extreme-right nationalists because it came to be related with a more fundamental problem: the Kurdish question. At the time the death penalty was discussed, the leader of the Kurdish movement, Abdullah Ocalan, was in prison under a death sentence. Despite the nationalists' objections, the law passed in the Parliament with the help of those who argued in favor of the abolition of capital punishment, including the sentence passed on Ocalan, and for the recognition of Kurdish rights in Turkey. It was a victory of reformers against nationalists. Turkish skeptics in Europe dismissed these reforms that they considered as only on paper and cosmetic, that is, superficial.

The third crucial moment was when the Turkish Parliament voted on March 1, 2003, and denied the United States' demand to attack Iraq from Turkish soil. Such a rupture of alliance with American politics in the Iraq War was unexpected and meant to be a turning point in Turkish-American relations. The motion was accepted by only half of the parliamentary vote. It represented the divide that many Turkish citizens felt inside themselves; they thought this war to be an unjust one, but they feared to harm the alliance with the United States. Besides, the antiwar manifestations were on the same wavelength with European peace movements. These movements mobilized in favor of peace rather than around arguments of religious fraternity. Turkey, long-term ally of the United States and candidate for membership in the EU, found itself in the divide between the two, at the fracture between the two Wests that appeared during the Iraq War. The European powers did not read the Turkish refusal of alliance with American politics as a sign of sharing "European peace sensibility" or maturation of democracy. However, the Arab intellectuals did; Turkey gained respectability in their eyes to the extent that it articulated a decision autonomous from the United States, and foremost, it relied on public opinion and parliamentary power to say no to American politics. As the Syrian intellectual Sadik Al-Azam has written, this Turkish stance was highly regarded by Arab nationalists and also won popularity for Turkey more widely among people who asked themselves: "What Arab king, president, or ruler could go to the president of the United States and tell him, 'My parliament rejected your government's request,' without the American president either laughing him off the stage, or even yelling back at him, 'Go to hell you and your parliament, we know what kind of an assembly you have at your disposal'?"[11] Turkey appeared to be a country capable of standing up to the United States and no longer willing to be seen as a regional American police force. Europeans, however, missed the democratic aspect of the decision. They suspected Turkey of having a hidden agenda to invade the north of Iraq and control the establishment of an autonomous Kurdish state and power. My point here is not to judge the plausibility of such arguments, although retrospectively speaking they appear to be untrue, but to point to the deficiency of European politics to hear and support the emerging democratic voices and thereby dismiss the very impact of European values of democracy.

The fourth topic to highlight on the stakes of democracy in Turkey concerns the Armenian question, which represents a major taboo for Turkish nationalism. The official view of the past is based on the suppression and denial of the 1915 genocide that created a sort of forced short-term memory and diffused amnesia of the past for generations of the Turkish Republic. Therefore, there are two aspects of the problem. One question is remembering the past, and the second is developing and expressing points of view that are independent of the official one. The choice of words to label the events, whether deportation, ethnic cleansing, massacres, or genocide, became a battleground in the public debate on the issue, which took place despite nationalist pressure and juridical intimidation. The debate was initiated by a few Turkish intellectuals and historians, including members of the Armenian community who challenged the ideological version of the events, defying the taboos of Turkish nationalism, exploring new ways of relating to the emotional trauma of the Armenians, and developing a new narrative on the historical past. In that respect, the Istanbul conference signaled a new period. The conference bringing together 219 Turkish historians, who wanted to pursue a free discussion on the Armenian past of Turkey in spite of pressures and postponement, was at last held at Bilgi University in September 2005.[12] It marked a collective effort to break away from the official discourse and to confront Turkish nationalism with its own past.

Alongside these historically constructed points of view that challenge the established ideology, there are also voices and images that bring forth past memory and engage a process of remembering. The postcards exhibition in Istanbul illustrating the lives of Armenians all over Turkey prior to the genocide was a case in point. The autobiographical book *My Grandmother*,[13] written by Fethiye Çetin, a female human rights lawyer, was another breakthrough in the public consciousness. She tells the story of her discovery of her grandmother's Armenian origins. The writer follows her grandmother's life, gives an account of past events, breaks the silence on the subject, and also brings for many other people the possibility of remembering and discovering their Armenian ascendance.

On April 23, 2014, Turkish Prime Minister Recep Tayyip Erdogan offered condolences for the first time for the mass killings of Armenians under Ottoman rule during the First World War. His comments came on the eve of the ninety-ninth anniversary of the mass deportation of Armenians in 1915. Erdogan described the events of 1915 as "our shared pain" and expressed hope that those who died were at peace. This meant a radical move away from the negationist politics of the Turkish Republic.

The presence of European perspective in Turkey worked against identity groups as it dismantled national myths. It is not a linear, peaceful process; it is an ongoing process and battle. In the eyes of many hard-line nationalists and secularists (*laïcards*), the European project in forcing Turkey in the direction of democratization and demilitarization endangers the stability of the country, opening up a gate for escalating demands of Kurdish nationalists and religious fundamentalists and the claims of Armenian diasporas.

I am trying not to argue, therefore, for a problem-free society but on the contrary to illustrate, by means of concrete but significant cases, the ways in which Turkish society faces its problems, tries to bring into public awareness matters that were kept out of sight, repressed, or forgotten, and frames them politically. The honor killings follow the same political pattern; that is, the issue is brought to public attention with the help of feminist organizations calling for new legislation. It is the way of politicizing the issues, carrying them from silenced arenas (silenced whether by shame or repression) and giving them plurality of voices and visibility in the public sphere, that describes the existence of a democratic pattern.

In France, a debate on the legitimacy of Turkish membership, as I have argued, started the moment Turkey accomplished most of the requirements, getting closer to standards set by the EU. Once again, one should note that it is the proximity, the encounter between the two, that is the source of conflict and controversy. Turkish membership triggered an anxiety of loss and a desire for boundary maintenance. In that respect, Europe entered into a quest for identity. Throughout these debates, Europe has contrived to protect an identity defined by shared history and common cultural values rather than building for the future. It is in areas outside its core countries (for instance in Spain, Portugal, and Greece) that Europe has more appeal as a project and the power to induce democratization. In Turkey, where Europeanness is not part of a natural historical legacy, it was appropriated voluntarily as a political project, as a perspective for change, as a frame for rethinking commonness and difference.

The debates over Turkey's candidacy revealed the difference between Europe perceived as a project in distinction from Europe as an identity. For European countries there is simply continuity, not difference, between the two: European unity is the European identity written large. Islamic presence in Europe reveals the tensions between universalism in Europe and its Judaeo-Christian legacy. European claims for universalism and its limits are tested and defied by Turkey's candidacy for membership as well as by Muslim migrants within Europe.

In the present situation, neither the experiment of Europe with Islam nor that of Muslims with democracy seems to be promising. In Turkey, the loss of the hegemony of the secular and the election of AKP initially contributed to the extension of democracy by integrating the pious classes into politics and by recognition of the rights of different ethnic, religious, and confessional minorities. However, during a decade in power, the AKP government has reduced democracy to Muslim majority rule and turned back to politics of polarization with authoritarian undertones. In Europe, the increasing popularity of far right parties has weakened the center right and socialist political traditions. The politics of resentment against Islam in Europe and the ban on Muslim actors' entry into public life deepen the cleavages with Muslim citizens. New forms of jihadism as a mixture of individual delinquency, piety, and political terrorism exacerbate politics of hate and fear. In addition to the rise of Islamophobia, the reemergence of anti-Semitism destroys the social tissue and threatens democratic politics and peace, the two precious legacies of Europe.

Old Europe as a Novel Experience?

Islam has become an agenda-setting issue for different national politics and countries of Europe, shaping the future of the EU. Obviously, the intersection between Europe and Islam is not a new phenomenon; there is a deep-rooted, long, and connected history of exchanges, wars, colonization, and waves of immigration that have profoundly shaped, in different periods of history, relations between Muslims and Europeans, including their traumas. Yet there is something novel in the contemporary mode of encounter between the two, including the ways old memories emerge in the present-day discourses.

At present, there is a two-way interactive relationship between Islam and Europe, and the proximity of the two engenders conflict. Neither Islam nor Europe presents itself as a homogeneous entity. Rather than stressing the inner differences, I have emphasized the processes of interaction through which both are transformed. It is the problematic zones of contact between the two that I wanted to bring to attention. The frontiers are considered to be zones of both contact and separation between different neighbor populations. But precisely because the European experience means the weakening or effacement of these frontiers, the process can be understood as "interpenetrations" between Muslims and Europeans. However, this does not imply a peaceful and nonviolent process. The asymmetry of desires underpins the encounter between the two and fuels the emotions; passion, fear, irrationality, anger, and hate become the ingredients of the debate and the conflict.

Muslims make their entry into the European public agenda in different ways, whether they claim for their religiosity as in the case of the headscarf movement, for European membership as in the case of Turkish candidacy, or for their social rights as in the case of suburban youth. It is by manifesting their differences that they become visible and disturbing to the public eye. They force their entry into spaces that were reserved for European white citizens. Muslims in Europe imply the infraction of boundaries that used to maintain the civilizational, national, or urban divide.

The novelty of the experience originates from the very location of this encounter. Europe is the place where the conversation and the confrontation take place in proximity to each other, and in the present time. The comfort of geographical distance is lost. In that respect, the old Europe is becoming a site of novel experiences where we can no longer speak of two distinct and separate civilizations in time and in space. Neither can it be traced solely at the political level of decision makers, governments, and nation-states. Islam becomes a public affair, meaning a concern for all. But the publicness refers also to an emerging problem, a process that carries ideas, opinions from the private, interior, personal to an outspoken, shared, circulated public idea. In that sense, we can speak of a growing public awareness of Islamic presence in Europe. The encounter between Europe and Islam is a two-way relationship that transforms both sides, both European and Muslim self-presentations. The project of European unity brings forth and reinforces a transnational aspect of connectivity. And last but not least, the naming of self and the other becomes a crucial and decisive matter that will define the outcome of this process. The ways in which Europe and Islam will connect to each other, create hyphenated identities, or on the contrary dress boundaries of separation will be decisive for the future of European Islam, French-Muslims, or Euro-Turks.[14]

These debates, precipitated by different problems, were framed and problematized in strikingly similar ways in European public and civic discourse. Turkish EU membership became an agenda-setting issue for European identity politics, while the headscarf debate provoked a larger debate on the secular egalitarian values of Europe. The very manner in which these debates have been framed creates a point of departure for viewing the making of Europe in its encounter with Islam.

In these zones of contact we can discern the hidden dynamics of the process: how these issues appeared in the public arena, how they were voiced by different public figures, and how they became part of a new European imaginary. In different ways, these public debates contributed to the problematization of the bond between European and Muslim identities. In the headscarf debate, the principle of republican secularism, laïcité, was mobilized as a mode of French exceptionalism. By contrast, a different set of values were mobilized (and interestingly, not secularism) in the debate over Turkish EU membership, so that the status of Europe as a distinct civilization and whether Turkey was properly considered part of Europe, as well as its geography, history, and religion, became a major issue. In these debates, we can observe how Turkey came to represent the other against whom European identity was reinforced and reconstructed while, concurrently, the Islamic headscarf was equated with gender oppression, against which emancipatory principles of feminism and secularism were interlaced as prerequisites of European citizenship.

Both cases deployed the trope of territory. Turkey as a territory of Islam implied an enlargement of European territory by her candidacy. Second- and third-generation Muslim migrants, distanced from their countries of origin, bring to public discourse their experiences of a denationalized Islam. The question of territory is also raised by their claims of Muslim visibility and presence in European territories and public spaces such as cities, schools, hospitals, and prisons. In relation to both the Turkish candidacy and headscarf debates, we witness a slide from a political to a religious overdetermination of the issue.

In both instances, anti-Americanism, in different ways, provided an anchor for the elaboration of a collective French and European self-presentation. In the case of the headscarf debate, communitarianism and multicultural liberalism—identified with Anglo-Saxon ways of dealing with difference—served as a model of opposition to the republican French universalism that is praised for enhancing the individual integration and public neutrality achieved by laïcité. In the case of Turkish EU membership, American pressure is not merely considered diplomatically unacceptable but criticized as suspect in its hidden and destructive intentions toward the European project. In both these debates, then, we witness a struggle to find ways of thinking Europeanness and self-presentation in contrast to America.

Europeanism appears as an identity defined by shared history and common cultural values rather than as a project for rethinking the political bond. Europe, as a project, offers a possibility of surpassing the fixity and purity of identities in favor of an intercultural social experience. Will the European project seize this opportunity or follow the lines of global cleavages?[15] It is an open, two-way question whose answer depends on both Muslims and Europeans.

Notes

Chapter 1: Public Sphere beyond Religious-Secular Dichotomies

1 Habermas, "On the Relations between the Secular Liberal State and Religion," 258.

2 See, especially, Rosati and Stoeckl, "Introduction."

3 Taylor, *A Secular Age.*

4 Göle, *Interpénétrations.*

5 Wallerstein et al., *Open the Social Sciences.*

6 Chakrabarty, *Habitations of Modernity.*

7 Among a series of publications on multiple modernities, see Eisenstadt, *Comparative Civilizations and Multiple Modernities,* and "Multiple Modernities"; Göle, "Islam in Public: New Visibilities and New Imaginaries"; Gaonkar, "On Alternative Modernities."

8 The notion of *différend,* developed by Lyotard, refers to a conflict that cannot be settled due to the absence of a ruling judgment applicable to both arguments under consideration. When two expressions "in a heterogeneous system are not translatable the one to the other, there is a différend between these expressions (or between the categories to which they belong), because they are heterogeneous." Différend applies not only to verbal expressions but also to silences that function as negations, to *phrase-affects.* I use this notion, going beyond the discursive domain, to indicate all the practices, forms, and norms that

seem to be untranslatable to European imaginaries and languages at this precise moment in time and which thus provoke controversies. See Lyotard, *Le différend*, 10–29.

9   For theoretical elaborations on the notion of controversy, see Göle, *Islam and Public Controversy in Europe*.

10 Fukuyama, "The End of History?"

11 Vidmar-Horvat and Delanty, "Mitteleuropa and the European Heritage."

12 Delanty, "The Making of a Post-Western Europe."

13 Gingrich, "Frontier Myths of Orientalism."

14 Rosati, "The Turkish Laboratory."

15 Huntington, *The Clash of Civilizations and the Remaking of World Order*, 74, 139–44.

16 Huntington, *The Clash of Civilizations and the Remaking of World Order*, 178.

17 Kuru, *Secularism and State Policies toward Religion*, 169.

18 Rosati, "The Turkish Laboratory."

19 Alexander, "The Arc of Civil Liberation."

20 Warner, *Publics and Counterpublics*.

21 Compagnon, *Les antimodernes*.

Chapter 2: Secular Modernity in Question

An earlier version of this chapter was published under the title "European Self-Presentations and Narratives Challenged by Islam : Secular Modernity in Question," in *Decolonising European Sociology: Transdisciplinary Approaches*, edited by Encarnación Gutiérrez-Rodríguez, Manuela Boatca, and Sérgio Costa (Farnham, UK: Ashgate, 2010).

1   Bakhtin, *Esthétique et théorie du roman*. Elsewhere, I propose adopting the Bakhtinian notion of chronotope in order to grasp the significance of Islam's anachronistic presence in the European public sphere. See Göle, "Thinking Islamic Difference in Pluralistic Democracies."

2   Chakrabarty, *Habitations of Modernity*; Ashcroft, *The Post-colonial Studies Reader*.

3   Wallerstein et al., *Open the Social Sciences*.

4   Dozon, "Le temps des retours."

5   For the notion of "presentism," see Hartog, *Régimes d'historicité*. Hartog locates the origins of presentism in the crumbling of the Berlin Wall and in the dissolution of the Soviet Union. For a discussion of Hartog's regime of historicity in the English language, see Lorenz, "Unstuck in Time or the Sudden Presence of the Past."

6   For the French and German controversies see Amir-Moazami, *Discourses and Counter-Discourses*; Bowen, *Why the French Don't Like Headscarves*; and Scott, *The Politics of the Veil*. For the British context, see Joppke, *Veil*.

7   See Roy, *L'Islam mondialisé*.

8   Göle, "Close Encounters."

9   Kepel, *Fitna*.

10 Khosrokhavar, *Les nouveaux martyrs d'Allah*.

11 Göle, "Islam in Public."

12 Taylor, *Modern Social Imaginaries*.

13 Anderson, *Imagined Communities*.

14 Calhoun, *Nations Matter*.

15 Allievi and Nielsen, *Muslim Networks and Transnational Communities in and across Europe*.

16 Göle, *Interpénétrations*.

17 Sassen, *Territory, Authority, Rights*.

18 Habermas, *Droit et démocratie*, and *Après l'Etat-nation*.

19 Quéré, "L'Espace public. "

20 Göle, *The Forbidden Modern*.

21 Vinas, *Entre oui et non*.

22 Göle, *Musulmanes et Modernes*.

23 Derrida, *L'Autre Cap*.

Chapter 3: Religious-Secular Frontiers

This chapter is a revised version of "Manifestations of the Religious-Secular Divide: Self, State, and the Public Sphere," in *Comparative Secularism in a Global Age*, edited by Linell E. Cady and Elizabeth Shakman Hurd (London: Palgrave Macmillan, 2010).

1 Gauchet, *La religion dans la démocratie*.

2 Taylor, *A Secular Age*, see especially, 230–35.

3 See Lewis, *What Went Wrong?*, and *The Crisis of Islam*.

4 Benhabib, "Democratic Iterations."

5 For the ways Islam becomes contemporaneous with Europe, see Göle, *Interpénétrations*.

6 One should not think that the historical genealogy of the secular in Turkey starts with Atatürk republicanism; some aspects of the secular are part of the Ottoman state tradition and Islamic historical legacy. In order to locate the origins of Turkish republican ideology in the Ottoman past and for the correction of dualistic representations of the secular and the religious, see Hanioğlu, *A Brief History of the Late Ottoman Empire*.

7 Göle, "La question de la femme," and "Secularism and Islamism in Turkey."

8 Gellner, "Religion and the Profane."

9 Khosrokhavar, "The Public Sphere in Iran."

10 Taylor, *Varieties of Religion Today*, 83.

11 Chakrabarty, *Habitations of Modernity*.

12 Sayyid, *A Fundamental Fear*.

13 Göle, "Islam, European Public Space, and Civility."

14 Greenblatt, *Renaissance Self-fashioning*; and Pieters, *Moments of Negotiation*.

15 Kuru, *Secularism and State Policies toward Religion*.

16 Turkey's ban on headscarves at universities dates back to the 1980s but was significantly tightened after February 28, 1997, when army generals with public support ousted a government they deemed too

Islamist. The ruling Justice and Development Party (AKP) attempted to lift the ban, a move that was cited as evidence when a closure case was filed against the party on grounds that it had become a focal point of "antisecular activities." After a series of efforts by the governing party in power since 2002, the prohibition of headscarves at universities was lifted in 2011. And, in October 2013, the headscarf prohibition was abolished for women working in state offices. However, the headscarf ban will remain in the military, police force, and judiciary, but government officials have hinted recently that it could soon be lifted. See the *New York Times* article on the subject, accessed October 1, 2014, http://www.nytimes.com/2013/10/09/world/europe/turkey-lifts-ban-on-head-scarves-in-state-offices.html?_r=0.

17 See Allievi, "Conflicts over Mosques in Europe"; and Avcıoğlu, "The Mosque and the European City."

Chapter 4: Web of Secular Power

This chapter is an expanded version of "The Civilizational, Spatial, and Sexual Powers of the Secular," in *Varieties of Secularism in a Secular Age*, edited by Michael Warner, Jonathan Vanantwerpen, and Craig Calhoun (Cambridge, MA: Harvard University Press, 2010).

1 For a very elaborate approach to the variety of theories, historical meanings, and Western/non-Western trajectories of secularity, see Gorski and Altinordu, "After Secularization?"

2 Asad, *Formations of the Secular.*

3 See Warner, Vanantwerpren, and Calhoun, "Introduction," 1–31.

4 Gauchet, *La religion dans la démocratie.*

5 Balibar, "Dissonances within Laïcité."

6 Asad, *Formations of the Secular.*

7 Asad, *Genealogies of Religion.*

8 For a comparison of secularism in France and Turkey, see Burdy and Marcou, eds., "Laïcité(s) en France et en Turquie."

9 See among others Göle, "Authoritarian Secularism"; Hurd, *The Politics*

of *Secularism in International Relations*; Kuru, *Secularism and State Policies toward Religion*.

10 On this affair, see Gaspard and Khosrokhavar, *Le foulard et la République*.

11 For a discussion of the report's presentation of a pluralistic opening in the interpretation of French laïcité, see Wallerstein, "Render unto Caesar?"

12 Scott, *The Politics of the Veil*, 97.

13 Scott, *The Politics of the Veil*, 102, 135.

14 For the charter of this collective created in reaction to the 2004 law, see their website, accessed on November 15, 2014, http://lmsi.net /Charte-des-collectifs-Une-ecole.

15 Emmanuel Terray qualified the debate as a "collective hysteria" to the extent that it became contagious, meaning that all positions went in the same direction, in favor of legislation to ban the headscarf. See Terray, "L'hystérie politique," 103–18.

16 For a comparative analysis of the debates, see Amir-Moazami, *Discourses and Counter-Discourses*.

17 Barkat, "La loi contre le droit."

18 See chapter 6, note 6.

19 See Casanova, *Public Religions in the Modern World*.

20 Gellner, *Muslim Society*, 68.

21 For the recent developments concerning the headscarf ban in Turkey, see chapter 2, note 16.

22 Goffman, *Frame Analysis*.

23 Goffman, *Stigma*.

24 See Balesescu, *Paris Chic, Tehran Thrills*.

25 Göle, "Secularism and Islamism."

26 Benhabib, "The Return of Political Theology."

27 The Association for the Support of a Modern Lifestyle (in Turkish, Çağdaş Yaşamı Destekleme Derneği) was created in 1989 by leading intellectual and professional women and became a fervent defender of secularism and gender equality. The association played a crucial

role against lifting the ban on wearing an Islamic headscarf in the universities in 2007 and 2008.

28 For the commemoration of the republican heritage, see Özyürek, *The Nostalgia for the Modern*.

29 Roy, *Globalized Islam*.

30 Jeanette Jouili inquired in France and Germany how Muslim women learned to be pious Muslims, by acquiring religious knowledge, cultivating bodily disciplines, and surveying their minds and bodies. See Jouili, "Devenir pieuse."

31 For an elaboration of the notions of space, publicness, and counterpublics in the cultural politics of displaying differences, see Warner, *Publics and Counterpublics*.

32 Jouili, "Devenir pieuse."

33 Calhoun, "Habitus, Field, and Capital."

34 Turner, *The Anthropology of Performance*, 24.

35 Taylor, *Varieties of Religion Today*.

36 Taylor, *A Secular Age*.

Chapter 5: The Gendered Nature of the Public Sphere

This chapter is an updated version of "Gendered Nature of the Public Sphere," *Public Culture* 10, no. 1 (1997).

1 Milani, *Veils and Words*, 238.

2 On social movements, see Touraine, *The Voice and the Eye*. For an approach to Islamism as a social movement, see Göle, "L'émergence du sujet Islamique."

3 For a detailed discussion on this dispute, see Olson, "Muslim Identity and Secularism in Contemporary Turkey." The same debate also exists in Western contexts, especially in France. See chapter 2 of this volume.

4 Diane Singerman shares this interest in linking women and politics. See Singerman, *Avenues of Participation*.

5 Ryan, "Gender and Public Access," 277.

6   For a comparison of secularism in France and Turkey, see Burdy and Marcou, "Laïcité(s) en France et en Turquie."

7   Dressler, *Writing Religion*.

8   Such a secularist and universalist concept of the public sphere is best elaborated in Habermas's work, *The Structural Transformation of the Public Sphere*. Today, efforts to include communitarian aspects, gender identities, class dimensions, and ethnicity expand the definition of the public sphere as a liberal bourgeois sphere and contribute to our understanding of the contemporary problems of democracy. See Calhoun, *Habermas and the Public Sphere*, and Benhabib, *Situating the Self*.

9   Burdy and Marcou, "Laïcité(s) en France et en Turquie," 13.

10 "Didactic secularism" was coined by Ernest Gellner to describe the Kemalist mode of secularism in Turkey. See Gellner, *Muslim Society*, 68.

11 Graham-Brown, *Images of Women*.

12 For criticism of superficial Westernization and of male characters in Turkish novels, see Mardin, "Super Westernization in the Ottoman Empire in the Last Quarter of the Nineteenth Century."

13 Karaosmanoğlu, *Ankara*, 129.

14 Later, from the 1980s on, feminist scholars and writers in Turkey would criticize women's identity defined within and by a nationalist project, paving the way for a new feminist consciousness. Works by Şirin Tekeli have pioneered the critical evaluation of the Kemalist reforms regarding women. See Tekeli, *Kadınlar ve Siyasal Toplumsal Hayat* and "Emergence of the New Feminist Movement in Turkey."

15 Arat, *The Patriarchal Paradox*.

16 Behar and Duben, *Istanbul Households*.

17 Bozdoğan, "The Predicament of Modernism in Turkish Architectural Culture."

18 The terms are taken from Afsaneh Najmabadi. See Najmabadi, "Hazards of Modernity and Morality."

19 Sivan, *Radical Islam*, 50–82.

20 Bourdieu, *Distinction*.

21 Göle, "Secularism and Islamism in Turkey."

22 Foucault, *The History of Sexuality*, 61.

23 Turner draws our attention to the dearth of attempts to spell out the differences between the Christian and Islamic notions of conscience. Turner, *Orientalism, Post-Modernism and Globalism*, 62.

24 For an elaborate discussion of these cases of blasphemy, see Kerrou, "Blasphème et apostasie en Islam."

25 Here, I follow Anderson's analysis of nationalism, applying it to Islamism. See Anderson, *Imagined Communities*.

26 Emile Durkheim long ago pointed out the two distinct realms, sacred and profane, each indispensable for the establishment and reproduction of the social tie.

27 For such an approach to the black public sphere, see Appadurai et al., "Editorial Comment."

28 Appadurai et al., "Editorial Comment."

29 Göle, *The Forbidden Modern*.

30 The emergence of a secular feminist movement in Turkey during the 1980s contributed to the proliferation of feminist writings. For a study of the radical feminist movement in Turkey, see Arat, "Women's Movement of the 1980s in Turkey," and Sirman, "Feminism in Turkey."

31 I studied new forms of Islamic public visibility with my undergraduate students at Boğaziçi University during the academic year 1995–96. See Göle, *Islamın Yeni Kamusal Yüzleri*.

32 Öncü, "Packaging Islam."

33 *Awra* (nakedness, shame) refers to the intimate parts of the human body that must be covered or concealed from the sight and/or hearing of strangers. Precisely which body parts must be considered awra varies among different schools of Islamic thought. See Benkheira, "Sexualité."

34 Efe, *Mızraksız İlmihal*.

35 Touraine, *Critique of Modernity*, 226–27.

36 Milani, *Veils and Words*, 201–2.

37 On how to read, analyze, and interpret contemporary "autobiographical voices" as ethnographical material, as constructions of self and

community, as revelations of traditions, re-collections of disseminated identities, and cultural criticism, see Fischer, "Autobiographical Voices (1, 2, 3) and Mosaic Memory."

38 Cohen and Arato use the term *self-limiting radicalism* to define the
pluralistic aspect of new Western social movements. See Cohen and
Arato, *Civil Society and Political Theory*, 493.

39 Çayır, *Islamic Literature in Contemporary Turkey*.

40 Kömeçoğlu, "New Sociabilities."

Chapter 6: Public Islam

An earlier version of this chapter was previously published in *Public
Culture* 14, no. 1 (2002).

1 For the definitions of Islamism, Islamist, and Muslim, see chapter 5 of
this volume.

2 Khosrokhavar and Roy, *Iran*; Adelkhah, *Etre moderne en Iran*.

3 Roy, *L'Echec de l'Islam politique*; Kepel, *Jihad*.

4 On historical semantics, see Koselleck, *Futures Past*.

5 Kaviraj, "Filth and the Public Sphere," 98.

6 Castoriadis, *The Imaginary Institution of Society*, 238.

7 Castoriadis, *The Imaginary Institution of Society*, 367–68.

8 Eisenstadt and Schluchter, "Introduction."

9 Göle, "Global Expectations, Local Experiences, Non-Western Modernities."

10 See Taylor, "Modern Social Imaginaries."

11 "The Revolt of Women," *Hürriyet*, May, 4 1999. According to a survey on
political and social values conducted in October 1999 by the Foundation of Political Science in Istanbul (IMV-SAM), 61 percent of the Turkish population thinks that Kavakçı should have taken off her headscarf while in the Parliament. Another covered woman deputy, from
the Nationalist Party (MHP), had taken off her headscarf to attend the
National Assembly and was applauded while giving her oath.

12 See Peres, *The Day Turkey Stood Still*.

13 "The Revolt of Women."

14 Peres, *The Day Turkey Stood Still.*

15 Frisby, *Fragments of Modernity*, 6.

16 Geertz, "Thick Description."

17 Revel, *Jeux d'échelles.*

18 Revel, *Jeux d'échelles*, 36. Revel uses this example to establish a parallelism with microhistory. Rather than privileging one scale of analysis over the other, he argues that the methodological principle should be the variations between them.

19 Göle, *The Forbidden Modern.*

20 For an analysis of the foreigner in terms of distance from and proximity to the social group through Simmel's notion of "l'étranger," see Simmel, "Digressions sur l'étranger"; for an English translation, see Wolff, *The Sociology of Georg Simmel.*

21 Tabboni, "Le multiculturalisme et l'ambivalence de l'étranger."

22 For global circulations and modern social imaginaries, see Appadurai, *Modernity at Large.*

23 Goffman, *Les cadres de l'expérience*, 417.

24 Turner, *The Anthropology of Performance*, 24.

25 The concept of *extramodernity* is developed in Göle, "Global Expectations."

26 On the public sphere in the West, see Habermas, *The Structural Transformation of the Public Sphere*; on the public sphere in a Muslim context, see chapter 5 of this book.

27 Lefebvre, *La production de l'espace*, 35.

28 Lefebvre, *La production de l'espace*, 121.

29 Benhabib, *Situating the Self.*

30 Martuccelli, *Sociologies de la modernité*, 447.

31 Touraine, *Critique of Modernity*, 337.

32 On reflexivity and modernity, see Beck, Giddens, and Lash, *Reflexive Modernization.*

33 For a discussion of such an approach to performing modernity in the case of the Miao population in China, see Schein, "Performing Modernity."

34 Warner, "Public and Private."

35 Goffman, *Behavior in Public Places*, 15.

36 Goffman, *Behavior in Public Places*, 93.

37 The title of the Turkish edition of my book on veiling, *The Forbidden Modern*, is *Modern Mahrem*.

38 Calhoun, "Habitus, Field, and Capital."

39 Sennett, *Flesh and Stone*.

40 Sennett, *Flesh and Stone*, 370.

41 Lash, *Another Modernity*, 4.

42 Castoriadis, *The Imaginary Institution of Society*, 367.

Chapter 7: Public Culture, Art, and Islam

An earlier version of this chapter was previously published in *Cultural Politics* 5, no. 3 (2009).

1 Gruzinski, *Quelle heure est-il là-bas?*, 36.

2 Gruzinski, *Quelle heure est-il là-bas?*, 57–59.

3 Huntington, *The Clash of Civilizations and the Remaking of World Order,* 138–51.

4 Huntington, *Who Are We?*

5 Arjomand, "Social Theory and the Changing World," 344–45.

6 What makes some words audible or public and not others? The words of the former French president would have been a nonissue had they not opened a Pandora's box and been followed by many other politicians, public spokespersons, historians, feminists, and the like, not only in France but across Europe, culminating in a series of political moves and decisions that made Turkish candidacy problematic, its legitimacy even being open to doubt. Turkey, which was declared as a candidate country for EU membership in 1999, faces the specter of a "third-way" proposal, a "special partnership" since 2008.

7 See Göle, "Identifier l'Europe, est-ce altériser la Turquie?"

8 Benedict XVI, "Papal Address at the University of Regensburg."

9 Edmund Burke and David Prochaska describe the shift in paradigm in thinking about the relationship between the West and the non-West

and present a rich historiographical review of the field since Edward Said's *Orientalism* was published. They show how the new readings of race and gender, and the role of visual culture have expanded the field in new directions. See Burke and Prochaska, "Introduction," 1–75.

10 Göle, *Interpénétrations*.

11 Göle, *Anverwandlungen*.

12 The exhibition-workshop was based on my concept *mahrem*. The curator of the exhibition Emre Baykal added artistic positions in visual media to my research into the "non-western modernities project." See Sabina Vogel's article, accessed on November 25, 2008, http://universes-in universe.org/eng/nafas/articles/2008/mahrem.

13 Casanova, "Immigration and the New Religious Pluralism," 65.

14 Modood, *Multiculturalism*.

15 *Islamophobia: Fact not Fiction* was the first study to use the term; it was conducted in Great Britain in 1997 by an antiracist association, the Runnymede Trust. In France it entered into the debates with the publication of Vincent Geisser's book, *La nouvelle Islamophobie*. Peter Gottschalk and Gabriel Greenberg argue that Islamophobia reflects a social anxiety toward Islam and Muslims that is not uniquely reserved to Europeans but also deeply ingrained in Americans; they examine these stereotypical images in American political cartoons. See Gottschalk and Greenberg, *Islamophobia*.

16 MacMaster and Lewis, "Orientalism."

17 Geulen, "Reflections on the History and Theory of the Public," 64.

18 Geulen, "Reflections on the History and Theory of the Public," 65.

19 Arendt, *The Human Condition*, 178.

20 D'Entreves, "Hannah Arendt."

21 Göle, *The Forbidden Modern*, 83–130.

22 Kenan Çayır depicts the emergence of personal and self-reflexive voices among young covered Muslim women authors in Turkey. See Çayır, "Islamic Novels."

23 Warner, *Publics and Counter-Publics*, 75.

24 Ammann, "Private and Public in Muslim Civilization."

25 Fischer, "Iran and the Boomeranging Cartoon Wars."

26 Appadurai, *Modernity at Large*, 47.

27 According to Rollason, "Walter Benjamin elaborates the motif of the 'constellation' as symbol of the relationship which emerges when the historian places a number of apparently unrelated historical events in significant conjuncture. The constellation links past events with each other, or else links past to present; its formation stimulates a flash of recognition, a quantum leap in historical understanding. For example, the French revolutions of 1789, 1830, and 1848 and the Paris Commune of 1870 would all be placed in a constellar relation, as events separated in time but linked by a common insurrectionary consciousness." See Rollason, "Walter Benjamin's Arcades Project and Contemporary Cultural Debate in the West," 283.

28 Rollason, "Walter Benjamin's Arcades Project and Contemporary Cultural Debate in the West," 262–96.

Chapter 8: Europe's Trouble with Islam

This chapter is based on an earlier version of "Europe's Encounter with Islam: What Future?," *Constellations* 13, no. 2 (2006).

1 The European Court of Human Rights was set up in Strasbourg in 1959 to deal with alleged violations of the 1950 European Convention on Human Rights. Recognition of the right of individual application was, however, optional, and it could therefore be exercised only against those states that had accepted it. Turkey ratified the right for individual applications from Turkish citizens to the European Commission of Human Rights in 1987; the compulsory judicial power of the European Court of Human Rights was recognized in 1989. Turkey has the highest number of applications to the court.

2 See Göle and Billaud, "Islamic Difference and the Return of Feminist Universalism."

3 See Bruma, *Murder in Amsterdam*.

4 See Scheffer, "The Multicultural Drama," and *Immigrant Nations*.

5 Paul, "Turkey's EU Journey," 122.

6 Guénif-Souilamas and Macé, *Les féministes et le garçon arabe.*

7 For a detailed discussion of the third, postimmigration phase, see Göle, "Introduction."

8 Elias, *La civilisation des mœurs*, 53–73.

9 See the *New York Times* story on the issue, "Ex-French President Snubs Turks on Union Bid," accessed on November 15, 2002, http://www.nytimes.com/2002/11/09/world/ex-french-president-snubs-turks-on-union-bid.html.

10 İsmet Özel, a well-known Islamist poet, considered observant Muslims in Turkey as "Turkey's blacks." For a study on Özel's work, see Morrison, "To Be a Believer in Republican Turkey."

11 Al-Azam, "Turkey, Secularism and the EU," 456.

12 See *Turkish Daily News* story, "Armenian Conference Finally Gets under Way at Bilgi University," accessed on September 26, 2005, http://www.hurriyetdailynews.com/default.aspx?pageid=438&n=armenian-conference-finally-gets-under-way-at-bilgi-university-2005-09-25.

13 Çetin, *Anneannem.*

14 See Kaya and Kentel, "Euro-Turks."

15 See Göle, "The Making and Unmaking of Europe in Its Encounter with Islam."

Bibliography

Adelkhah, Fariba. *Etre moderne en Iran*. Paris: Karthala, 1998.

Al-Azam, Sadik J. "Turkey, Secularism and the EU: A View from Damascus." *Philosophy and Social Criticism* 37, no. 4 (2011): 449–59.

Alexander, Jeffrey C. "The Arc of Civil Liberation: Obama-Tahrir-Occupy." Paper presented at the Reset-Dialogues Istanbul Seminars 2012 (The Promises of Democracy in Troubled Times), Istanbul Bilgi University, May 19–24, 2012.

Allievi, Stefano. "Conflicts over Mosques in Europe: Between Symbolism and Territory." In *Islam and Public Controversy in Europe*, edited by Nilüfer Göle, 69–82. London: Ashgate, 2014.

Allievi, Stefano, and Jorgen S. Nielsen, eds. *Muslim Networks and Transnational Communities in and across Europe*. Boston: Brill, 2003.

Amir-Moazami, Schirin. "Discourses and Counter-Discourses: The Islamic Headscarf in the French and German Public Spheres." PhD diss., European University Institute, Department of Political and Social Sciences, Florence, 2004.

Ammann, Ludwig. "Private and Public in Muslim Civilization." In *Islam in Public: Turkey, Iran, and Europe*, edited by Nilüfer Göle and Ludwig Ammann, 77–125. Istanbul: Bilgi University Press, 2006.

Anderson, Benedict. *Imagined Communities: Reflections on the Origins and Spread of Nationalism*. New York: Verso, 1991.

Appadurai, Arjun. *Modernity at Large*. Minneapolis: University of Minnesota Press, 1996.

Appadurai, Arjun, Carol A. Breckenridge, Lauren Berlant, and Manthia Diawara. "Editorial Comment: On Thinking the Black Public Sphere." *Public Culture* 7 (1994): xii–xiii.

Arat, Yeşim. *The Patriarchal Paradox: Women Politicians in Turkey*. Toronto: Associated University Presses, 1989.

Arat, Yeşim. "Women's Movement of the 1980s in Turkey: Radical Outcome of Liberal Kemalism?" In *Reconstructing Gender in the Middle East: Tradition, Identity, and Power*, edited by Fatma Göçek and Shiva Balaghi, 100–112. New York: Columbia University Press, 1994.

Arendt, Hannah. *The Human Condition*. Chicago: University of Chicago Press, 1958.

Arjomand, Saïd Amir. "Social Theory and the Changing World: Mass Democracy, Development, Modernization and Globalization." *International Sociology* 19, no. 3 (2004): 321–54.

Asad, Talal. *Formations of the Secular: Christianity, Islam, Modernity*. Stanford, CA: Stanford University Press, 2003.

Asad, Talal. *Genealogies of Religion*. Baltimore: Johns Hopkins University Press, 1993.

Ashcroft, Bill, ed. *The Post-colonial Studies Reader*. London: Routledge, 1994.

Avcıoğlu, Nebahat. "The Mosque and the European City." In *Islam and Public Controversy in Europe*, edited by Nilüfer Göle, 57–68. London: Ashgate, 2014.

Bakhtin, Mikhaïl. *Esthétique et théorie du roman*. Translated by Daria Olivier. Paris: Gallimard, 1978.

Balesescu, Alexandru. *Paris Chic, Tehran Thrills*. Bucharest: Zeta Books, 2007.

Balibar, Étienne. "Dissonances within Laïcité." *Constellations* 11, no. 3 (2004): 353–67.

Barkat, Sidi Mohammed. "La loi contre le droit." In *Le foulard islamique en questions*, edited by Charlotte Nordmann, 28–37. Paris: Editions Amsterdam, 2004.

Beck, Ulrich, Anthony Giddens, and Scott Lash. *Reflexive Modernization: Politics, Tradition, and Aesthetics in the Modern Social Order*. Cambridge: Polity, 1994.

Behar, Cem, and Alain Duben. *Istanbul Households: Marriage, Family and Fertility 1880–1940*. Cambridge: Cambridge University Press, 1991.

Benedict XVI. "Papal Address at the University of Regensburg." *Zenit: The World Seen from Rome*, September 12, 2006. Accessed on May 17, 2014. http://www.zenit.org/article-16955?1 =english.

Benhabib, Seyla. "Democratic Iterations: The Local, the National and the Global." In *Another Cosmopolitanism: Hospitality, Sovereignty and Democratic Iterations*, edited by Robert Post, 147–86. Oxford: Oxford University Press, 2006.

Benhabib, Seyla. "The Return of Political Theology: The Scarf Affair in Comparative Constitutional Perspective in France, Germany, and Turkey." *Dignity in Adversity: Human Rights in Turbulent Times*, 166–83. Malden, MA: Polity Press, 2011.

Benhabib, Seyla. *Situating the Self: Gender, Community, and Postmodernism in Contemporary Politics*. New York: Routledge, 1992.

Benkheira, Muhammed Hocine. "Sexualité." In *Dictionnaire du Coran*, edited by M. A. Amir-Moezzi, 815–18. Paris: Editions Robert Laffont, 2007.

Bourdieu, Pierre. *Distinction*. Cambridge, MA: Harvard University Press, 1984.

Bowen, John R. *Why the French Don't Like Headscarves: Islam, the State, and Public Space*. Princeton, NJ: Princeton University Press, 2007.

Bozdoğan, Sibel. "The Predicament of Modernism in Turkish Architectural Culture: An Overview." In *Rethinking Modernity and National Identity in Turkey*, edited by Sibel Bozdogan and Resat Kasaba, 133–56. Seattle: University of Washington Press, 1997.

Bruma, Ian. *Murder in Amsterdam: The Death of Theo van Gogh and the Limits of Tolerance*. New York: Penguin, 2006.

Burdy, Jean-Paul, and Jean Marcou, eds. "Laïcité(s) en France et en Turquie." *Cemoti* 19 (1995): 5–34.

Burke, Edmund, III, and David Prochaska. "Introduction: Orientalism from Postcolonial Theory to World Theory." In *Genealogies of Orientalism: History, Theory, Politics,* edited by Edmund Burke and David Prochaska, 1–75. Lincoln: University of Nebraska Press, 2008.

Calhoun, Craig, ed. *Habermas and the Public Sphere.* Cambridge, MA: MIT Press, 1992.

Calhoun, Craig. "Habitus, Field, and Capital: The Question of Historical Specificity." In *Bourdieu: Critical Perspectives,* edited by Craig Calhoun, Edward LiPuma, and Moishe Postone, 61–89. Chicago: University of Chicago Press, 1993.

Calhoun, Craig. *Nations Matter: Culture, History and the Cosmopolitan Dream.* New York: Routledge, 2007.

Casanova, José. "Immigration and the New Religious Pluralism: A European Union/United States Comparison." In *Democracy and the New Religious Pluralism,* edited by Thomas Banchoff, 59–85. New York: Oxford University Press, 2007.

Casanova, José. *Public Religions in the Modern World.* Chicago: University of Chicago Press, 1994.

Castoriadis, Cornelius. *The Imaginary Institution of Society.* Translated by Kathleen Blamey. Cambridge: Polity, 1987.

Çayır, Kenan. *Islamic Literature in Contemporary Turkey: From Epic to Novel.* New York: Palgrave Macmillan, 2007.

Çayır, Kenan. "Islamic Novels: A Path to New Muslim Subjectivities." In *Islam in Public: Turkey, Iran, and Europe,* edited by Nilüfer Göle and Ludwig Ammann, 191–227. Istanbul: Bilgi University Press, 2006.

Çetin, Fethiye. *Anneannem.* Istanbul: Metis, 2004.

Chakrabarty, Dipesh. *Habitations of Modernity: Essays in the Wake of Subaltern Studies.* Chicago: University of Chicago Press, 2002.

Cohen, Jean L., and Andrew Arato. *Civil Society and Political Theory.* Cambridge, MA: MIT Press, 1992.

Compagnon, Antoine. *Les antimodernes: De Joseph de Maistre à Roland Barthes.* Paris: Gallimard, 2005.

Delanty, Gerard. "The Making of a Post-Western Europe: A Civilizational Analysis." *Thesis Eleven* 72 (2003): 8–25.

D'Entreves, Maurizio Passerin. "Hannah Arendt." In *The Stanford Encyclo-*

pedia of Philosophy, edited by Edward N. Zalta. Stanford, CA: Stanford University Press, 2008.

Derrida, Jacques. *L'autre cap*. Paris: Les Editions de Minuit, 1991.

Dozon, Jean-Pierre. "Le temps des retours." In *Les sciences sociales en mutation*, edited by Michel Wieviorka, 371–78. Paris: Editions Sciences Humaines, 2007.

Dressler, Marcus. *Writing Religion: The Making of Turkish Alevi Islam*. New York: Oxford University Press, 2013.

Efe, Mehmet. *Mızraksız İlmihal*. Istanbul: Yerli Yayınlar, 1993.

Eisenstadt, Shmuel Noah. *Comparative Civilizations and Multiple Modernities*. Leiden: Brill, 2003.

Eisenstadt, Shmuel Noah. "Multiple Modernities." *Daedalus* 129, no. 1 (2000): 1–29.

Eisenstadt, Shmuel N., and Wolfgang Schluchter. "Introduction: Paths to Early Modernities: A Comparative View." *Daedalus* 127, no. 3 (1998): 4–7.

Elias, Norbert. *La civilisation des mœurs*. Paris: Agora, 1973.

Fischer, Michael M. J. "Autobiographical Voices (1, 2, 3) and Mosaic Memory: Experimental Sondages in the (Post) modern World." In *Autobiography and Postmodernism*, edited by Kathleen M. Ashley et al., 79–129. Amherst: University of Massachusetts Press, 1994.

Fischer, Michael M. J. "Iran and the Boomeranging Cartoon Wars: Can Public Spheres at Risk Ally with Public Spheres Yet to Be Achieved?" *Cultural Politics* 5 (2009): 27–63.

Foucault, Michel. *The History of Sexuality*, vol. 1. Translated from the French by Robert Hurley. New York: Vintage Books, 1990.

Frisby, David. *Fragments of Modernity: Theories of Modernity in the Work of Simmel, Kracauer, and Benjamin*. Cambridge: Polity, 1985.

Fukuyama, Francis. "The End of History?" *National Interest* (summer 1989): 3–18.

Gaonkar, Dilip Parameshwar. "On Alternative Modernities." *Public Culture* 11, no. 1 (1999): 1–18.

Gaspard, Françoise, and Farhad Khosrokhavar. *Le foulard et la République*. Paris: La Découverte, 1995.

Gauchet, Marcel. *La religion dans la démocratie: Parcours de la laïcité*. Paris: Gallimard, 1998.

Geertz, Clifford. "Thick Description: Toward an Interpretative Theory of Culture." *The Interpretation of Cultures: Selected Essays*. New York: Basic Books, 1973.

Geisser, Vincent. *La nouvelle Islamophobie*. Paris: La Decouverte, 2007.

Gellner, Ernest. *Muslim Society*. Cambridge, MA: Cambridge University Press, 1981.

Gellner, Ernest. "Religion and the Profane." *Eurozine* Articles, 2000. Accessed on May 25, 2014. http://www.eurozine.com/articles/2000–08 -28-gellner-en.html.

Geulen, Christian. "Reflections on the History and Theory of the Public." In *Islam in Public: Turkey, Iran, and Europe*, edited by Nilüfer Göle and Ludwig Ammann, 45–77. Istanbul: Bilgi University Press, 2006.

Gingrich, Andre. "Frontier Myths of Orientalism: The Muslim World in Public and Popular Cultures of Central Europe." In *Mediterranean Ethnological Summer School*, edited by B. B. Baskar and B. Burmen, 99–128. Ljubljana: Institute for Multicultural Research, 1998.

Goffman, Erving. *Behavior in Public Places: Notes on the Social Organization of Gatherings*. New York: Free Press, 1966.

Goffman, Erving. *Les cadres de l'expérience*. Paris: Minuit, 1991.

Goffman, Erving. *Frame Analysis: An Essay on the Organization of Experience*. New York: Harper and Row, 1974.

Goffman, Erving. *Stigma: Notes on the Management of Spoiled Identity*. New York: Touchstone, 1963.

Göle, Nilüfer. *Anverwandlungen: Der Islam in Europa*. Translated by Ursel Schafer. Berlin: Verlag Klaus Wagenbach, 2008.

Göle, Nilüfer. "Authoritarian Secularism and Islamic Participation: The Case of Turkey." In *Civil Society in the Middle East*, vol. 2, edited by A. Richard Norton, 17–44. Leiden: Brill, 1996.

Göle, Nilüfer. "Close Encounters: Islam, Modernity, and Violence." In *Understanding September 11*, edited by Craig Calhoun, P. Price, and A. Timmers, 332–44. New York: New Press, 2002.

Göle, Nilüfer. "L'émergence du sujet islamique." In *Penser le sujet autour d'Alain Touraine*, edited by François Dubet and Michel Wieviorka, 221–35. Paris: Fayard, 1995.

Göle, Nilüfer. *The Forbidden Modern: Veiling and Civilization*. Ann Arbor: University of Michigan Press, 1996.

Göle, Nilüfer. "The Gendered Nature of the Public Sphere." *Public Culture* 10 (1977): 61–81.

Göle, Nilüfer. "Global Expectations, Local Experiences, Non-Western Modernities." In *Through a Glass, Darkly: Blurred Images of Cultural Tradition and Modernity over Distance and Time*, edited by Wil Arts, 40–55. Boston: Brill, 2000.

Göle, Nilüfer. "Identifier l'Europe, est-ce altériser la Turquie?" *Confluences Méditerranée* 52 (2004–5): 55–63.

Göle, Nilüfer. *Interpénétrations: L'Islam et l'Europe*. Paris: Galaade Editions, 2005. Translated by Steven Rendall as *Islam in Europe: The Lure of Fundamentalism and the Allure of Cosmopolitanism* (Princeton, NJ: Marcus Weiner, 2010).

Göle, Nilüfer. "Introduction: Islamic Controversies in the Making of European Public Spheres." In *Islam and Public Controversy in Europe*, edited by Nilüfer Göle, 3–20. London: Ashgate, 2014.

Göle, Nilüfer. "L'Islam à la rencontre des sciences sociales." In *Les sciences sociales en mutation*, edited by Michel Wieviorka, 417–26. Paris: Editions Sciences Humaines, 2007.

Göle, Nilüfer. "Islam, European Public Space, and Civility." *Eurozine*, 2007. Accessed on June 15, 2014. http://www.eurozine.com/articles/2007–05 –03-gole-en.html.

Göle, Nilüfer. "Islam in Public: New Visibilities and New Imaginaries." *Public Culture* 14 (2002): 173–90.

Göle, Nilüfer, ed. *İslamın Yeni Kamusal Yüzleri: İslam ve Kamusal Alan Üzerine Atölye*. Istanbul: Metis, 2000.

Göle, Nilüfer. "The Making and Unmaking of Europe in Its Encounter with Islam: Negotiating French Republicanism and European Islam." In *Varieties of World-Making beyond Globalization*, edited by Nathalie Karagiannis and Peter Wagner, 173–90. Liverpool: Liverpool University Press, 2007.

Göle, Nilüfer. *Musulmanes et modernes: Voile et civilisation en Turquie.* [1993]. Paris: La Découverte, 2003.

Göle, Nilüfer. "La question de la femme, le républicanisme et la laïcité: Regards croisés entre la Turquie et la France." In *Islam de France, Islams d'Europe*, 101–10. Paris: L'Harmattan, 2005.

Göle, Nilüfer. "Secularism and Islamism in Turkey: The Making of the Elites and Counter-elites." *Middle East Journal* 51, no. 1 (1997): 46–58.

Göle, Nilüfer. "Thinking Islamic Difference in Pluralistic Democracies." In *Difference and Democracy: Exploring Potentials in Europe and Beyond*, edited by Kolja Raube and Annika Sattler, 159–81. Hamburg: Campus Verlag, 2011.

Göle, Nilüfer, and Ludwig Amman, eds. *Islam in Sicht: Der Auftritt von Muslimen im öffentlichen Raum.* Bielefeld, Germany: Transcript, 2004. Also published as *Islam in Public* (Istanbul: Bilgi University Press, 2006).

Göle, Nilüfer, and Julie Billaud. "Islamic Difference and the Return of Feminist Universalism." In *European Multiculturalisms: Cultural, Religious and Ethnic Challenges*, edited by Anna Triandafyllidou, Tariq Modood, and Nasar Meer, 116–44. Edinburgh: Edinburgh University Press, 2011.

Gorski, Philip S., and Ateş Altınordu. "After Secularization?" *Annual Review of Sociology* 34 (2008): 55–85.

Gottschalk, Peter, and Gabriel Greenberg. *Islamophobia: Making Muslims the Enemy.* Lanham, MD: Rowman and Littlefield, 2008.

Graham-Brown, Sarah. *Images of Women: The Portrayal of Women in Photography of the Middle East, 1860–1950.* New York: Columbia University Press, 1988.

Greenblatt, Stephen. *Renaissance Self-Fashioning: From More to Shakespeare.* Chicago: University of Chicago Press, 1980.

Gruzinski, Serge. *Quelle heure est-il là-bas? L'Amérique et l'Islam à l'orée des temps modernes.* Paris: Seuil, 2008.

Gruzinski, Serge. *What Time Is It There? The Americas and Islam at the Dawn of Modern Times.* Cambridge: Polity Press, 2010.

Guénif-Souilamas, Nacira, and Eric Macé. *Les féministes et le garçon arabe.* Paris: Éditions de l'Aube, 2006.

Habermas, Jürgen. *Après l'état-nation: Une nouvelle constellation politique.* Translated by Rainer Rochlitz. Paris: Fayard, 2002.

Habermas, Jürgen. *Droit et démocratie: Entre faits et normes.* Translated by R. Rochlitz and C. Bouchindhomme. Paris: Gallimard, 1992.

Habermas, Jürgen. "On the Relations between the Secular Liberal State and Religion." In *Political Theologies: Public Religions in a Post-secular World,* edited by Hent de Vries and Lawrence E. Sullivan, 251–60. New York: New York University Press, 2006.

Habermas, Jürgen. "Religion in the Public Sphere." *European Journal of Philosophy* 14, no. 1 (2006): 1–25.

Habermas, Jürgen. *The Structural Transformation of the Public Sphere.* Cambridge, MA: MIT Press, 1991.

Hanioğlu, Şükrü. *A Brief History of the Late Ottoman Empire.* Princeton, NJ: Princeton University Press, 2008.

Hartog, François. *Régimes d'historicité.* Paris: Seuil, 2003.

Huntington, Samuel P. *The Clash of Civilizations and the Remaking of World Order.* New York: Simon and Schuster, 1996.

Huntington, Samuel P. *Who Are We? The Challenges to America's National Identity.* New York: Simon and Schuster, 2004.

Hurd, Elizabeth Shakman. *The Politics of Secularism in International Relations.* Princeton, NJ: Princeton University Press, 2008.

Joppke, Christian. *Veil: Mirror of Identity.* Malden, MA: Polity, 2009.

Jouili, Jeanette S. "Devenir pieuse: Femmes musulmanes en France et en Allemagne entre réforme de soi et quête de reconnaissance." PhD diss., Ecole des Hautes Etudes en Sciences Sociales, Paris, 2007.

Karaosmanoğlu, Yakup Kadri. *Ankara.* [1934]. Istanbul: Iletisim, 1983.

Kaviraj, Sudipta. "Filth and the Public Sphere: Concepts and Practices about Space in Calcutta." *Public Culture* 10 (1997): 83–113.

Kaya, Ayhan, and Ferhat Kentel. "Euro-Turks: A Bridge or a Breach between Turkey and the European Union? A Comparative Study of German-Turks and French-Turks." In EU-Turkey Working Papers, no.

14 (January 2005). Accessed on February 3, 2006. http://www.ceps.be /node/1035.

Kepel, Gilles. *Fitna, guerre au cœur de l'Islam*. Paris: Gallimard, 2004.

Kepel, Gilles. *Jihad: Expansion et déclin de l'islamisme*. Paris: Gallimard, 2000.

Kerrou, Mohamed. "Blasphème et apostasie en Islam." In *Monothéismes et modernités*, edited by Mohamed Kerrou, 177–204. Carthage: OROC (Orient-Occident) and Friedrich-Nauman Stiftung, 1996.

Khosrokhavar, Farhad. *Les nouveaux martyrs d'Allah*. Paris: Flammarion, 2003.

Khosrokhavar, Farhad. "The Public Sphere in Iran." In *Islam in Public: Turkey, Iran, and Europe*, edited by Nilüfer Göle and Ludwig Ammann, 257–80. Istanbul: Bilgi University Press, 2006.

Khosrokhavar, Farhad, and Olivier Roy. *Iran: Comment sortir d'une révolution religieuse*. Paris: Seuil, 1999.

Kömeçoğlu, Uğur. "New Sociabilities: Islamic Cafés in Istanbul." In *Islam in Public: Turkey, Iran, and Europe*, edited by Nilüfer Göle and Ludwig Ammann, 163–91. Istanbul: Bilgi University Press, 2006.

Koselleck, Reinhart. *Futures Past: On the Semantics of Historical Time*. New York: Columbia University Press, 1985.

Kuru, Ahmet T. *Secularism and State Policies toward Religion: United States, France, and Turkey*. Cambridge: Cambridge University Press, 2009.

Lash, Scott. *Another Modernity, a Different Rationality*. Oxford: Blackwell, 1999.

Lefebvre, Henri. *La production de l'espace*. Paris: Éditions Anthropos, 1986.

Lewis, Bernard. *The Crisis of Islam: Holy War and Unholy Terror*. New York: Modern Library, 2003.

Lewis, Bernard. *What Went Wrong? Western Impact and Middle Eastern Response*. New York: Oxford University Press, 2002.

Lorenz, Chris. "Unstuck in Time or the Sudden Presence of the Past." In *Performing the Past: Memory, History, and Identity in Modern Europe*, edited by Karin Tilmans, Frank van Vree, and Jay Winter, 67–104. Amsterdam: Amsterdam University Press, 2010.

Lyotard, Jean François. *Le différend*. Paris: Editions de Minuit, 1983.

MacMaster, Neil, and Toni Lewis. "Orientalism: From Unveiling to Hyper-veiling." *Journal of European Studies* 28 (1998): 121–35.

Mardin, Şerif. "Super Westernization in the Ottoman Empire in the Last Quarter of the Nineteenth Century." In *Turkey: Geographic and Social Perspectives*, edited by Peter Benedict et al., 403–30. Leiden: Brill, 1974.

Martuccelli, Danilo. *Sociologies de la modernité: L'itinéraire du XXᵉ siècle*. Paris: Gallimard, 1999.

Milani, Farzaneh. *Veils and Words: The Emerging Voices of Iranian Women Writers*. Syracuse, NY: Syracuse University Press, 1992.

Modood, Tariq. *Multiculturalism*. Cambridge: Polity, 2007.

Morrison, Scott. "To Be a Believer in Republican Turkey: Three Allegories of Ismet Özel." *Muslim World* 96, no. 3 (2006): 507–21.

Najmabadi, Afsaneh. "Hazards of Modernity and Morality: Women, State and Ideology in Contemporary Iran." In *Women, Islam and the State*, edited by Deniz Kandiyoti, 48–76. Philadelphia: Temple University Press, 1991.

Olson, Emilie. "Muslim Identity and Secularism in Contemporary Turkey: The Headscarf Dispute." *Anthropological Quarterly* 58, no. 4 (1985): 161–71.

Öncü, Ayşe. "Packaging Islam: Cultural Politics on the Landscape of Turkish Commercial Television." *Public Culture* 8 (1995): 51–71.

Özyürek, Esra. *The Nostalgia for the Modern: State Secularism and Everyday Politics in Turkey*. Durham, NC: Duke University Press, 2006.

Paul, Amanda. "Turkey's EU Journey: An Extraordinary Tale." *Arches Quarterly* 4, no. 8 (2011): 120–25.

Peres, Richard. *The Day Turkey Stood Still: Merve Kavakci's Walk into the Turkish Parliament*. Reading, UK: Garnet Publishing, 2012.

Pieters, Jürgen. *Moments of Negotiation: The New Historicism of Stephen Greenblatt*. Amsterdam: Amsterdam University Press, 2001.

Quéré, Louis. "L'espace public: De la théorie politique à la métathéorie sociologique." *Quaderni* 18 (1992): 75–92.

Revel, Jacques. *Jeux d'échelles: La micro-analyse à l'expérience*. Paris: Gallimard/Seuil, 1996.

Rollason, Christopher. "Walter Benjamin's Arcades Project and Contemporary Cultural Debate in the West." In *Modern Criticism*, edited by Christopher Rollason and Rajeshwar Mittapalli, 262–96. New Delhi: Atlantic Publishers, 2002.

Rosati, Massimo. "The Turkish Laboratory: Local Modernity and the Postsecular in Turkey." In *Multiple Modernities and Postsecular Societies*, edited by Massimo Rosati and Kristina Stoeckl, 61–78. London: Ashgate, 2012.

Rosati, Massimo, and Kristina Stoeckl. Introduction. *Multiple Modernities and Postsecular Societies*, 1–16. London: Ashgate, 2012.

Roy, Olivier. *L'echec de l'Islam politique*. Paris: Seuil, 1992.

Roy, Olivier. *Globalized Islam: The Search for a New Ummah*. London: Hurst, 2004.

Roy, Olivier. *L'Islam mondialisé*. Paris: Seuil, 2002.

Ryan, Mary P. "Gender and Public Access: Women's Politics in Nineteenth-century America." In *Habermas and the Public Sphere*, edited by Craig Calhoun, 259–88. Cambridge, MA: MIT Press, 1993.

Sassen, Saskia. *Territory, Authority, Rights: From Medieval to Global Assemblages*. Princeton, NJ: Princeton University Press, 2006.

Sayyid, Bobby S. *A Fundamental Fear: Eurocentrism and the Emergence of Islamism*. London: Zed, 1997.

Scheffer, Paul. *Immigrant Nations*. Cambridge: Polity, 2011.

Scheffer, Paul. "The Multicultural Drama." *NRC Handelsblad*, January 29, 2000.

Schein, Louisa. "Performing Modernity." *Cultural Anthropology* 14, no. 3 (1999): 361–95.

Scott, Joan W. *The Politics of the Veil*. Princeton, NJ: Princeton University Press, 2007.

Sennett, Richard. *Flesh and Stone: The Body and the City in Western Civilization*. New York: W. W. Norton, 1996.

Simmel, Georg. "Digressions sur l'étranger." In *L'école de Chicago: Naissance de l'écologie urbaine*, edited by Yves Grafmeyer and Isaac Joseph. Paris: Editions du Champ Urbain, 1979.

Singerman, Diane. *Avenues of Participation*. Princeton, NJ: Princeton University Press, 1995.

Sirman, Nükhet. "Feminism in Turkey: A Short History." *New Perspectives on Turkey* 3 (1989): 1–34.

Sivan, Emmanuel. *Radical Islam*. New Haven, CT: Yale University Press, 1985.

Tabboni, Simonetta. "Le multiculturalisme et l'ambivalence de l'étranger." In *Une société fragmentée? Le multiculturalisme en débat*, edited by Michel Wieviorka et al., 239–40. Paris: La Découverte, 1997.

Taylor, Charles. *Modern Social Imaginaries*. Durham, NC: Duke University Press, 2004.

Taylor, Charles. "Modern Social Imaginaries." *Public Culture* 14, no. 1 (2002): 91–124.

Taylor, Charles. *A Secular Age*. Cambridge, MA: Harvard University Press, 2007.

Taylor, Charles. *Varieties of Religion Today: William James Revisited*. Cambridge, MA: Harvard University Press, 2002.

Tekeli, Şirin. "Emergence of the New Feminist Movement in Turkey." In *The New Women's Movement: Feminism and Political Power in the USA*, edited by Drude Dahlerup, 179–99. London: Sage, 1986.

Tekeli, Şirin. *Kadınlar ve Siyasal Toplumsal Hayat* [Women and political social life]. Ankara: Birikim, 1982.

Terray, Emmanuel. "L'hystérie politique." In *Le Foulard islamique en questions*, edited by Charlotte Nordmann, 103–18. Paris: Editions Amsterdam, 2004.

Touraine, Alain. *Critique of Modernity*. Translated by David Macey. Oxford: Blackwell, 1995.

Touraine, Alain. *The Voice and the Eye: An Analysis of Social Movement*. Cambridge: Cambridge University Press, 1981.

Turner, Bryan S. *Orientalism, Post-Modernism and Globalism*. London: Routledge, 1994.

Turner, Victor. *The Anthropology of Performance*. New York: PAJ, 1986.

Vidmar-Horvat, Ksenija, and Gerard Delanty. "Mitteleuropa and the European Heritage." *European Journal of Social Theory* 11, no. 2 (2008): 203–18.

Vinas, Florence T. *Entre oui et non: Simmel, Philosophe de l'Ame moderne, La parure et autres essais.* Paris: Editions Maison des Sciences de l'Homme, 1998.

Wallerstein, Immanuel, ed. *Open the Social Sciences: Report of the Gulbenkian Commission on the Restructuring of the Social Sciences.* Stanford, CA: Stanford University Press, 1996.

Wallerstein, Immanuel. "Render unto Caesar? The Dilemmas of a Multicultural World." *Sociology of Religion* 46, no. 2 (2005): 121–33.

Warner, Michael. "Public and Private." *Publics and Counterpublics*, 21–65. Cambridge, MA: Zone, 2002.

Warner, Michael. *Publics and Counterpublics.* Cambridge, MA: Zone, 2002.

Warner, Michael, J. Vanantwerpen, and C. Calhoun. Introduction. *Varieties of Secularism in a Secular Age*, 1–31. Cambridge, MA: Harvard University Press, 2010.

Wolff, Kurt H., ed. *The Sociology of Georg Simmel.* New York: Free Press, 1950.

Index

259

261